A People's History of Quebec

Jacques Lacoursière and Robin Philpot

A People's History
of Quebec

Baraka
Books

Baraka Books and Les éditions du Septentrion thank the Canada Council for the Arts for the support provided for the translation of this book from French to English.

Éditions du Septentrion thanks the Canada Council for the Arts and the Société de développement de entreprises culturelles du Québec (SODEC) for the support provided to its publishing program, and the Government of Québec for its Programme de crédit d'impôt pour l'édition de livres. We also acknowledge the financial assistance of the Government of Canada through its Canadian Book Publishing Development Program.

Cover: Samuel de Champlain's 1632 map of New France, in *Les Voyages de la Nouvelle France occidentale dicte Canada.*
Inset from left to right: Port of Montreal in 19th century, based on lithography by Duncan, Toronto Public Libarary; Battle of Saint-Eustache, 1837, National Archives of Canada; René Lévesque at victory celebration, November 15, 1976.

Library and Archives Canada Cataloguing in Publication

Lacoursière, Jacques, 1932-

A people's history of Quebec / Jacques Lacoursière and Robin Philpot; translated by Robin Philpot.

Translation of Une histoire du Québec.

Includes index.

ISBN 978-0-9812405-0-3

1. Québec (Province) - History. I. Philpot, Robin II. Title.

FC2911.L3413 2009   971.4
C2009-903650-9

Legal Deposit – 3rd quarter 2009
Bibliothèque et Archives nationales du Québec
Library and Archives Canada

Translation and adaptation by Robin Philpot
6th printing

© Baraka Books   © Les éditions du Septentrion 1992
6977, rue Lacroix   835, avenue Turnbull
Montréal, Québec   Québec, Québec
H4E 2V4   G1R 2X4
Telephone: 514-808-8504   www.septentrion.qc.ca
info@barakabooks.com
www.barakabooks.com

Original first edition: *Une histoire du Québec racontée par Jacques Lacoursière*, Septentrion 2002.

Trade Distribution & Returns
LitDistCo
C/o 100 Armstrong Ave.
Georgetown, ON
L7G 5S4
Ph: 1-800-591-6250
Fax: 1-800-591-6251
orders@litdistco.ca

Contents

Map of New France by Samuel de Champlain, published in Paris in 1632. When the Kirke brothers, privateers from Dieppe, captured the "habitation" at Quebec, Champlain returned to Europe and struggled to ensure that France recovered its colony. This map was published to support his work.

CHAPTER 1

Hard Slow Beginnings

The history of Quebec began formally on Friday, July 24, 1534. Ship captain Jacques Cartier sent his seamen ashore at the end of the Gaspé Peninsula to erect a cross bearing an escutcheon with three fleurs-de-lis and a plate where it was engraved "Vive le roi de France." Jacques Cartier described the scene in his log. "Once the cross was raised, we knelt down and joined hands before it in worship." The French visitors used signs to explain what the ceremony was about and pointed to the heavens above "whence cometh our redemption."

Cartier's Iroquoian hosts did not realize that in fact the cross-raising ceremony was a formal way of claiming possession of their land on behalf of the King of France. Nor did they know that the Europeans believed they could take over any portion of land that did not already belong to a Christian Sovereign. Their chief Donnacona sensed nonetheless that something serious was amiss. For Donnacona and his people "Mother Earth" belonged to everybody and these visitors from France had not requested permission to erect the cross. When Donnacona paddled out to meet the French ship, he insisted that the land belonged to them and that Cartier should have asked for permission. Cartier's answer was a half truth, but a whole lie. He claimed that the cross was nothing more than a beacon indicating the entry to the harbour.

Cartier then brought two of Chief Donnacona's sons on board and, as was the custom, took them back to France to prove he had reached new lands.

Jacques Cartier, who was long considered to have "discovered" Canada, was not really the first European to reach what is now known as Quebec. For decades French, English, Portuguese, Spanish, Basques, and Northern Europeans had fished cod on the grand banks off Newfoundland. Cod was a staple for all Catholics. In those days Catholics were bound to abstinence for 140 days every year. Eating meat was a mortal sin on those days and fish was the only substitute allowed.

Long before Europeans had ever reached the continents to which they gave the name America in 1507, the land had been inhabited for tens of thousands of years. The St. Lawrence Valley was settled a little later than elsewhere since it took longer for the glaciers to melt and for the Champlain Sea to recede. Depending on the region, archaeological research shows human occupation of the land dating back eight to ten thousand years.

The two Iroquois people Cartier brought to France sparked considerable interest, especially when they were paraded before the King's Court. They soon learned the rudiments of French and were astonished by the way Europeans raised their children. Corporal punishment was commonplace in France whereas children in Aboriginal North American society were never reprimanded physically.

Jacques Cartier set out in 1535 on a second expedition to what Europeans considered to be the "New World." His two Aboriginal guests—or captives—spoke of a river that would take him deep into the interior of the continent. As for other explorers, he hoped to find a route to China, the land of spices the value of which had shot up after the Ottomans had seized Constantinople in the middle of the 15th century.

The French sailed upriver as far as Stadacona, later to be called Quebec. Stadacona was at the heart of a region known as the "Kingdom of Canada," with "Canada" being a place name of Iroquoian origin meaning a village or group of houses. After a brief visit to the large Aboriginal town of Hochelaga on the island of Montreal, Cartier and his men settled in to face the rigours of their first North American winter. Early in May 1536 before weighing anchor for France, he erected another cross with the French coat of arms and the Latin inscription, "François I reigning by the grace of God, King of the French." This was in fact a second claim to possession of the land.

Along with the Spanish and the Portuguese who had established settlements in America, the French hoped to settle the St. Lawrence Valley. In 1541, Jacques Cartier was appointed second in command to Jean-François de La Rocque, sieur de Roberval, and they crossed the Atlantic again bringing hundreds of settlers with them, many of whom came straight from prison. Cartier returned hastily to France however, believing that the gold and diamonds he had in his ship would be proof of the riches in the New World. Roberval had reached Newfoundland by then and was preparing to sail upriver. This second attempt to settle was also doomed to fail and the failure was compounded by the fact that Cartier's "riches" were nothing but fool's gold and quartz.

Thus ended the first chapter in the history of the formal French presence in Quebec. More than half a century went by before other plans were hatched to settle the St. Lawrence River Valley. Lack of a settlement did not mean however that the St. Lawrence was abandoned during that period. The Basques and the French continued to conduct fur trading and fishing expeditions, and rivalry was intense. In 1587, for instance, two of Jacques Cartier's great-nephews, Jean and

Michel Noël, were confronted with competing traders along the river.

At the turn of the 17th century the riches in New France were attracting more and more merchants and investors. King Henri IV, who ruled France from 1589 to 1610, set his sights on establishing a colony in the New World. In 1598, he granted letters patent to Troilus de La Roche de Mesgouez making him "lieutenant general of the countries of Canada, Newfoundland, Labrador and Norembègue." His efforts to establish a settlement on Sable Island failed, as did those of Pierre de Chauvin de Tonnetuit at Tadoussac in 1600. Tadoussac is located on the north shore of the St. Lawrence at the mouth of the Saguenay River. Attempts to settle Saint Croix Island located near the New Brunswick-Maine border were equally unsuccessful. French presence at Port-Royal, in Acadia, was also sporadic, and only when a fur trading post was opened at Quebec did it become possible to maintain a permanent settlement.

When the English settled in Virginia 1607, they represented a potential threat to Acadia, but more importantly they jeopardized the French fur trade monopoly. This prompted Pierre Du Gua de Monts to opt for another site to establish a small colony that would be closer to the inland source of fur supplies. He identified the Quebec Point on the north shore of the St. Lawrence as the ideal spot and instructed his lieutenant Samuel de Champlain to sail to the place where the St. Lawrence River narrows and, with a team of men, build a small settlement. They started building a group of houses on July 3, 1608, and later they would fortify them. The Basques, who worked out of Tadoussac, were not pleased at all and perceived the permanent upstream settlement as a threat to trade. They managed to convince some of Champlain's men to try to assassinate him but the plot failed and a conspirator named Jean Duval was hanged. During the first winter in Quebec scurvy ravaged the tiny settlement killing 20 of Champlain's 28-man crew.

When Champlain first travelled to Canada in 1603, he promised the Montagnais of Tadoussac, now known as the Innu, to help them wage war against the Iroquois. Six years later, he had to keep that promise. With two other men, Champlain travelled to Iroquoisia and crossed a lake that later would bear his name. When the French became allies of the Algonquins and the Hurons, they also became undying enemies of the Iroquois. Thus began almost a century of conflict, war, and tense relations punctuated only rarely by short periods of peace. It would nonetheless have been unthinkable at the time for Champlain to forsake the Aboriginal nations with whom he traded furs only to ally himself with others who lived far away. Although 60 years earlier Jacques Cartier had encountered Iroquoians living in the areas of Quebec and Montreal, none were left in the St. Lawrence River Valley when Champlain arrived. They had been replaced by Algonquian nations. Disease and wars undoubtedly explain the disappearance of the Iroquoians from this area.

Quebec was little more than a fur trading post for at least a decade and in an aim to find new sources of supply Champlain began to explore other areas. Only gradually did he become convinced that the new settlement could develop into the hub of a major French colony in North America. The monopoly holders were not happy when the first settler and his family arrived in 1617, but the context remained unchanged. Champlain believed that France had to establish a colony in North America or else England and Holland would scramble to set up colonies of their own in the St. Lawrence Valley.

The colony he envisioned was quite different from those that the English and Spanish were developing in the so-called

New World. Champlain and is mentor François Gravé, sieur du Pont, had a dream of harmony with the peoples he met whom he treated as equals, never doubting their humanity as others did. Champlain told the Montagnais or Innu: "our young men will marry your daughters and henceforth we shall be one people." Despite clashes with the Mohawks and Onondagas, his vision informs the history of New France, and it prompted 19th century New England historian Francis Parkman to observe that "Spanish civilization crushed the Indian; English civilization scorned and neglected him; French civilization embraced and cherished him." More recently in his book *Champlain's Dream*, historian David Hackett Fischer pointed out that his dream was that of "a new world as a place where people of different cultures could live together in amity and concord." The alliances established thereafter compensated for the small number of settlers and were the key to French success in North America.

In France, Cardinal Richelieu, Louis XIII's leading minister, decided in 1627 to see personally to the well-being of the small colony. He created the Company of New France made up of about one hundred associates who obtained a monopoly on the fur trade allowing them to fund the Company's activities, and most importantly to bring some 4,000 men and women settlers to Canada over the next 15 years. Many incentives were offered to encourage the French to emigrate and settle in the St. Lawrence Valley. These included three years of guaranteed food and lodging and the possibility for tradesmen to earn the title of master, which would be valid in France, in return for six years spent plying the trade in the colony. Cardinal Richelieu was in a pitched battle with Protestants at that time and so he decreed that only Catholics were entitled to settle in New France. Jews were also not allowed to settle there.

Recruitment of new settlers flourished so well that 400 people set sail for Quebec in spring 1628. France and England had been at war for a year and ships on the open seas were known to exchange fire and engage in battle. When the four ships carrying the settlers entered the mouth of the St. Lawrence off shore from Rimouski, they were attacked and defeated. The battle was extremely costly for the Company of New France that had invested a large portion of its assets in the expedition.

David, Thomas, and Lewis Kirke at the helm of the English ships demanded that Champlain capitulate. Champlain bluntly refused, but Quebec was forced to surrender in 1629, and became an English trading post for three years. Ironically, by the time the Kirke brothers seized Quebec, the two mother countries had already signed a peace agreement three months earlier. The colony was only returned to France in 1632.

In an effort to meet commitments to settle the new colony, the Company of New France resorted to a different approach for granting lands. In 1634 Robert Giffard was granted the seigneury to be known as Beauport that had one league of river frontage (about four kilometres) and stretched a league and a half inland. It was up to the new seigneur to grant lots to new settlers that he was responsible for recruiting. Many seigneuries were established and that was how the land was settled. This method, which marked a break with feudalism in France, became a feature in the development of much of Quebec.

Since rivers provided the main lines of travel and communication, most seigneuries had frontage on them. Long, rectangular lots were granted, usually about three arpents wide (approximately 180 metres) by 20 to 40 arpents deep (1200 to 2400 metres). Travelling upstream on the St. Lawrence still leaves one with the impression of a single long village stretching from Quebec City to Montreal along both sides of the river.

Under the seigneurial regime, both the seigneur and the censitaires (the grantees who in turn paid an annual rent or "cens") had rights and duties. The seigneur had to possess and live in a dwelling on the seigneury and build a communal mill where the censitaires could grind their grain. Every fourteenth bushel went to the seigneur, who was to be treated with honour. If the seigneur failed to settle his seigneury however, he could lose it. The land grant contract specified the number of days of work detail to which the censitaires were bound. The colonial administration could also conscript the seigneur on certain days for specific work details. Many people in France were inspired by the hope of obtaining land under such good conditions and so they heeded the call to settle in New France where life would surely be much freer than in the mother country.

Champlain ordered that a new trading post be built upstream at Trois-Rivières in the same year Giffard obtained his seigneury at Beauport and brought in his first settlers to settle on it. This new post also offered another target for Iroquois raiding parties.

As the population grew and with many people hoping to convert the Aboriginal people to Christianity, religious orders began to expand to New France. The Récollet Brothers were the first in 1615, but they lost their permission in 1632. The Jesuits on the other hand first appeared in 1625, and remained steadily except for the hiatus of the English occupation of Quebec. The Jesuits began offering classical education in the colony as of 1635, the year Champlain died. Four years later the first Ursuline Sisters landed and saw to the education of the young French and Aboriginal girls. That same year, in 1639, the Hospitaller Sisters opened Hôtel-Dieu, the first hospital in the colony.

The Counter-Reformation in France was like a tonic for Catholicism, inspiring many to undertake the mission to evangelize Aboriginal peoples. They joined forces in the Notre-Dame Society of Montreal with the aim of establishing a mystical colony on the island of Montreal located upstream from the Trois-Rivières trading post. The first group of settlers led by Paul de Chomedey de Maisonneuve reached Quebec in fall 1641, too late to go further upstream to the planned destination. By this time the Iroquois were already launching raids on selected targets. Charles Huault De Montmagny, the first man appointed Governor of New France, tried to convince Maisonneuve to settle on Île d'Orléans, a location less vulnerable to Iroquois raids. The leader of the "Montréalistes," as they liked to be called, flatly refused. On May 17, 1642 this small group landed on the island of Montreal and founded Ville-Marie, a name that illustrates the mystical aspirations of the founders of Montreal. The city was placed under the protection of the Virgin Mary.

Ville-Marie became a state within the state that bucked efforts by the governor of New France in Quebec to impose his authority over the new settlement. Maisonneuve on the other hand was disappointed to see Ville-Marie developing so slowly. Seeing that new blood and many new settlers were required, he decided to go to France himself. "I shall try to bring two hundred men [...] to defend the place," declared Maisonneuve; "if I have less than one hundred, I will not return because the settlement will be unsustainable." He sailed back in fall 1653 with 120 people. His trip became known as "La Grande Recrue," or the great recruitment. Among the recruits was Marguerite Bourgeoys, who would take charge of teaching the children of Ville-Marie. Marguerite Bourgeoys founded the Congregation of Notre-Dame de Montréal to assist her in carrying out her mission, but also to ensure the survival of the colony.

Iroquois raids marked the 1650s and resulted in dozens of casualties. Control of the fur trade was the source of the conflict, with the Iroquois wanting to be the only middlemen operating between the French and the fur suppliers. They strived to gain the upper hand over the Montagnais, Hurons, and Algonquins, and any other nation wanting a share of the trade. It should be remembered that the fur trade drove the economy of the young colony and that any interruption in supply would have dire consequences. In the late 1650s, for example, the Iroquois raids had almost brought fur shipments to Montreal and Quebec to a complete halt. According to Mother Superior Mary of the Incarnation of the Ursuline Sisters, the authorities seriously considered abandoning the colony and repatriating all the settlers to France. In summer 1660 a group of young Montréalistes led by Adam Dollard Des Ormeaux saved the colony from bankruptcy. They protected some 60 canoes manned by 300 members of the Ottawa nation and guided by Pierre-Esprit Radisson and Médard Chouart des Groseilliers. Their intervention allowed the fur traders to reach Ville-Marie unscathed with enough furs to keep the trade alive.

The situation remained extremely precarious. French authorities had no choice but to take all means necessary to save their North American colony. The regency of young King Louis XIV was ending and it was hoped that the reign of the new King would be beneficial to New France.

Inset of a map published in 1715. The scene was inspired by an illustration of Niagara Falls in Louis Hennepin's account. The beaver was given all the qualities of human beings.

Samuel de Champlain was an enigmatic person. Very well rounded, he combined courage, vision, determination, and skill, particularly in cartography.

CHAPTER 2

A Royal Colony

New France reached a watershed in 1663 when King Louis XIV decided to personally take control of his North American colony. He instructed his minister Jean-Baptiste Colbert to pay particular attention to Canada, referring only to the St. Lawrence Valley. Had he said New France he would have been referring to Acadia, which included the modern provinces of Nova Scotia, New Brunswick, Prince Edward Island, and Newfoundland, and to the Pays-d'en-Haut, or Upper Country, which encompassed the entire Great Lakes hinterland. A governor continued to head the colony but an intendant assisted him. An intendant had powers equivalent to those of the ministers of Finance, Justice, and Trade. The governor was responsible for raising an army for war but the intendant had to finance it. This two-headed leadership was completed by a sovereign council comprising the governor and the bishop and five councillors appointed by the two ex officio members. The sovereign council became the highest tribunal in the colony. This reform effectively dissolved the Company of New France.

The two serious problems that required immediate attention were the pacification of the Iroquois and the growth of the colony. The Marquis Alexandre de Prouville de Tracy, "lieutenant general of all the lands that belong to Us in Northern and Middle America including the mainland, the islands, and the rivers, etc..." was ordered to set sail for Quebec and wage war on the Iroquois. The Carignan-Salières regiment under the command of Henri de Chastelard, Marquis of Salières, comprised 24 companies with a total of some 1200 men. They landed at Quebec and stayed from mid-June to mid-September 1665. Their first task was to build a series of forts on the banks of the Richelieu River and on an island on Lake Champlain, which was the Iroquois' favourite route. In the presence of such an imposing military force, three of the five Iroquois nations signed a peace agreement. In winter 1665-66, an expedition to pacify the two other nations, the Mohawks and the Oneidas, failed. The following summer another expedition set out, but the Mohawks and Oneidas received advanced warning and fled. Their villages and their fields were razed. Seeing that the French outweighed them militarily, the two Iroquois nations reached a peace agreement with the French that held for another 18 years.

Intendant Jean Talon, acting on the orders of King Louis XIV's leading minister Jean-Baptiste Colbert, began insisting that soldiers and officers settle in the colony. Soldiers were promised land while officers were promised seigneuries. A third of the troops, exactly 403 people, took up the offer. Laval University historian Marcel Trudel summarized the offer made to the troops: "The plan was to give them land and help them settle by providing food supplies and tools and paying for their seeds for the first two arpents [1.7 acres] that they would clear and burn. In return, the soldiers would do the same for two more arpents that would be granted to new families arriving from France."

The population of the colony grew rapidly in the second half of the 1660s. According to the census reconstituted by Marcel Trudel, the colony had a population of 4219 men and women in 1666. Men greatly outnumbered women mainly because they had been signed up as soldiers, generally for a period of three years. As a result the 1663 figures show that for every woman in the colony there were six unmarried men. A certain balance was achieved when "marryable girls" began to arrive. Some girls would come with their families, others alone, but all would have a dowry. For others, the King provided the dowry. They were known as the "filles du roi" or the King's daughters. Many of these girls came directly from the Salpêtrière, which was the Paris General Hospital. The King's daughters numbered about 850 and arrived in Quebec between 1663 and 1673.

Believing that boys and girls should marry young, Louis XIV signed an edict on April 5, 1669 decreeing "that pecuniary fine be introduced, to be applied by the local hospitals, directed against fathers who failed to marry their male children by the age of 20 and their female children by the age of 16." The following year hardened bachelors were threatened with "losing numerous and varied freedoms to hunt, fish, and trade with the Savages and, if necessary, an even greater fine," should they fail to marry within a certain period of time. To encourage them to have many children, the Intendant established a sort of family allowance system: "In the future, the inhabitants of the said country who have up to 10 living children born in wedlock, among whom none was a priest, a nun or in a religious order, will be paid by the Kingdom in the said country a pension of 300 pounds a year each, and those who have 12 children will receive 400 pounds."

Gender equilibrium was achieved by 1673 making it no longer necessary to import more "marryable girls." The population of the colony had reached about 6700, which was tiny in comparison with the 120,000 inhabitants in the colonies of New England. Intendant Jean Talon realized that his dream of "making Canada into a grand and powerful state" did not please authorities in France. Colbert pointed out that "it would not be wise to depopulate the Kingdom of France as would be required in order to populate Canada." Disappointed, Jean Talon replied: "I shall no longer have the honour to speak to you of the grand establishment that I previously said could be made of Canada to the glory of the King and the benefit of his State, since you know that in old France there are not enough supernumeraries and unnecessary subjects to populate New France."

Those who decided to settle down in the Canadian part of New France, namely the St. Lawrence Valley, began to identify themselves as being different from French visitors. They became "Canadois" or "Canadiens." Research by historian Gervais Carpin indicates that the new identity slowly appeared in the 1660s. These "Canadiens" preferred to be called "habitants" instead of "paysans" or peasants as they were in France. Proximity with Aboriginal nations rapidly influenced their way of life. In a book published in 1664, the Governor of Trois-Rivières Pierre Boucher wrote: "People travel over the snow using a type of shoe made by the Savages known as 'raquettes' or snowshoes, and they are very helpful." Canoes also become necessary for navigating the rivers and lakes. The coureurs de bois could never have developed the fur trade without using canoes and snowshoes.

Louis XIV's minister Colbert pressured Intendant Jean Talon to make the Aboriginal people into French. He wrote telling him to "try to civilize the Algonquins, the Hurons and the other Savages who have embraced Christianity to prepare them to come and live as a community with the French and to live with them and according to their customs." However, as Mary of the Incarnation observed: "It is easier to make a Savage out of a Frenchman than to do the opposite."

Philosopher Henry David Thoreau would echo this observation after visiting Quebec in 1850. The *Canadiens* "reminded me of the Indians, whom they were slow to displace and to whose habits of life they themselves more readily conformed than the Indians to theirs." Thoreau cited Swedish-Finnish botanist Pehr Kalm who recounted his visit to New France as follows: "Though many nations imitate the French customs, yet I observed, on the contrary, that the French in Canada, in many respects, follow the customs of the Indians, with whom they converse every day. They make use of the tobacco-pipes, shoes, garters, and girdles of the Indians. They follow the Indian way of making war with exactness; they mix the same things with tobacco; they make use of Indian bark-boats, and row them in the Indian way; they wrap square pieces of cloth round their feet instead of stockings; and have adopted many other Indian fashions." Thoreau concluded: "The French, to their credit be it said, to a certain extent respected the Indians as a separate and independent people, and spoke of them and contrasted themselves with them as the English have never done."

With the help of the Aboriginal nations, the French led a series of expeditions during which they often took possession of the land. These expeditions also enabled them to explore North America and expand New France. In the presence of fourteen Aboriginal nations at Sault-Sainte-Marie, which is the junction point of the upper Great Lakes, Simon-François Daumont de Saint-Lusson officially claimed possession of a huge area of land on behalf of the King of France in June 1671. "In the name of the most high, most mighty and most redoubtable monarch Louis, the XIVth of the name, most Christian King of France and Navarre, we take possession of the said place of Ste Mary of the Falls as well as of Lakes Huron and Supérieur, the Island of Caientoton and of all other Countries, rivers, lakes and tributaries, contiguous and adjacent thereunto, as well discovered as to be discovered, which are bounded on the one side by the Northern and Western Seas and on the other side by the South Sea, including all its length or breadth." It is unlikely that he fully grasped the size of the land mass he had claimed.

With similar grandeur, a year earlier King Charles II of England had granted the land known to the French as the Northern Sea to his cousin Prince Rupert and the Company of Adventurers of England, later to be known as the Hudson's Bay Company. It included "all those Seas Streightes Bayes Rivers Lakes Creekes and Soundes in whatsoever Latitude they shall bee that lye within the the entrance of the Streightes commonly called Hudsons Streightes together with all the Landes Countryes and Territoryes upon the Coastes and Confynes of the Seas Streightes Bayes Lakes Rivers Creekes and Soundes aforesaid which are not now actually possessed by any of our Subjectes or by the Subjectes of any other Christian Prince or State." Real possession however requires effective occupation of the land, so these two land claims had the effect of drawing the lines of a vast battlefield in North America between France and England.

Expeditions to the south and the west of the colony did not immediately lead to problems with the authorities in New England. The explorers were intent on finding a new route to China and Japan, expanding New France, and opening new lands for the fur trade. The Canadian Louis Joliet and the Jesuit Missionary Jacques Marquette thus set out in 1673 in search of the famous Mississippi River that their Aboriginal allies spoke so eagerly about. Aboriginal guides facilitated their penetration into what were unknown lands for them. They descended the "father of waters" as far as the current border between Arkansas and Louisiana and made an important discovery when they established that the Mississippi did not flow to the California side of the continent. René-Robert

Cavelier de La Salle was the first explorer to reach the mouth of the Mississippi, and on April 9, 1682 he claimed possession of Louisiana in the name of the King of France. Although Louisiana covered an enormous territory, it failed to impress Louis XIV who, on learning of La Salle's exploit, sneered that "the discovery of Sieur de La Salle is perfectly useless." Quebec had nonetheless become the heart of a vast empire which continues to be illustrated by the thousands of place names that have survived in the Mississippi, Missouri, and Great Lakes watersheds. Although many of the names have been anglicized in spelling or pronunciation, it was the French explorers and settlers in the 17th and 18th centuries or their descendants hailing from Quebec City and Montreal who left us with names such as Detroit, Des Moines, Ouisconsin (Wisconsin), Illinois, Lake Superior, Isle Royale, Panis (Pawnees), Nadessioux (Sioux), Grand Marais, Duluth, St. Louis, the Capital City of South Dakota Pierre, the Capital City of Idaho Boise or Boisé, and so many more.

The "heart" of New France was threatened in 1689 when another war broke out between France and England. The peace that had reigned between the colony and the Iroquois had already been shattered two years earlier. Governor Jacques-René de Brisay de Denonville had schemed and captured about 40 Iroquois chiefs and sent them off to be galley slaves on French ships plying the Mediterranean. The Iroquois negotiated for the support and assistance of New England authorities and then attacked the little town of Lachine as soon as they heard that war had resumed. Lachine was key to the fur trade since it was the starting point for trips to the supply regions in the Pays-d'en-Haut or Upper Country. The English colonies, whose population was upwards of 160,000, were calling for the complete conquest and reduction of Canada, a country that counted a mere 10,700 inhabitants.

Louis de Buade, count of Frontenac, who had been Governor of New France from 1672 to 1682, returned seven years later with a specific plan to conquer New York and deport the Protestant population. That plan was never carried out. Having brought back the surviving Iroquois galley slaves with him, he hoped that the five Iroquois nations would not attack the French settlements. Early in the 1690s three military expeditions set out for New England. The *Canadiens* with their Aboriginal allies wreaked death and terror throughout New England. This prompted Cotton Mather, a Boston Puritan best known for his role in the Salem witch trials, to preach in favour of a crusade against the inhabitants of the St. Lawrence Valley. His rallying cry, "Canada must be reduced," left no doubt as to his ultimate goal.

The plans to retaliate involved sending a 32-ship fleet up the St. Lawrence to capture Quebec, while deploying an army down the Richelieu River to stymie Montreal before turning to attack the capital of New France from the west. While the fleet was sailing to Quebec, however, disease incapacitated the army. Admiral William Phips and his ships reached destination on October 16, 1690, anchored just offshore from Quebec, and immediately ordered Governor Frontenac to capitulate. Governor Frontenac had a feeling for drama and retorted to the English emissary: "My only reply to you will be from the mouth of my cannons; he must understand that one does not give orders like that to a man like me. He only has to do his best, as I shall do my best." The second siege of Quebec thus began. Although some engagements ensued, Admiral Phips feared the harsh winter on the ship and so he weighed anchor and set sail before winter set in.

In the hope of reducing the Iroquois, Governor Frontenac destroyed some villages in the Great Lakes region. During the same period, Pierre Le Moyne d'Iberville led a group of men who almost managed to chase the English out of Hudson Bay where the best and most abundant furs were to be found because of the cold weather. They also ravaged English settlements on Newfoundland. A peace treaty signed at Ryswijk in Holland put an end to hostilities and restored the situation as it was before the war, with all gains and losses being annulled. Iberville's battles thus left no lasting impact.

The French and Aboriginal nations were tired of the war and the tensions that had plagued both for decades. The hostilities had decimated both the Iroquois and the Aboriginal nations allied with France, but European-imported epidemics and particularly smallpox had decimated them even more so. Colonial authorities knew perfectly well that peace alone was the key to the survival of Canada. The economy was also swamped by a surplus of furs that threw the Company of Canada, which held a monopoly on the fur trade, into dire financial straits. Louis-Hector de Callière took over as Governor of New France after Frontenac died and hoped to bring both friendly and hostile Aboriginal nations to reach a lasting peace with France. This development haunted New England. Negotiations began in Montreal in summer 1700 and were very successful. French or Canadian ambassadors were sent out to meet other nations in distant lands and invite them to another peace conference in Montreal. In the summer of 1701, representatives of some 40 Aboriginal nations travelled by canoe to Montreal. They came from the entire Great Lakes region, from Baie verte (Green Bay) on the west side of Lake Michigan and Chécago (Chicago) on the southern tip, to Baie du tonnerre (Thunder Bay) on the northwest side of Lake Superior. Others came from the upper Mississippi Valley and from what is now northern New York State. Most were Algonquian nations, but the Iroquois also played an important role, and particularly the Huron leader Kondiaronk, who died the day before the treaty was signed. Celebrations and diplomatic ceremonies began on July 21 and lasted until August 7. As the delegations arrived, they paid a courtesy visit to the Mohawk at Kahnawake, the pro-French Iroquois community strategically located on the river route upstream from Montreal. When the peace treaty was signed with the French on August 4, 1701, some 1300 representatives of the 40 nations had set up camp in Montreal.

It was agreed that the Governor of New France would mediate any disputes that arose. The five Iroquois nations undertook to remain neutral should war break out again between France and England. (During the War of Conquest 50 years later, however, the Iroquois decided to side with the English following strategic intervention by William Johnson.) When France and England went to war again in September 1701 over succession to the Spanish throne, the Abenakis along with the Canadians raided settlements in New England. No Aboriginal nations raised a hand to stop them since the English were not signatories to Great Peace or Grand Settlement of Montreal of 1701. Moreover, the peace of 1701 made it possible for France to establish new settlements inland including Detroit.

War over succession to the Spanish throne had little impact on the St. Lawrence River Valley. Acadia however was the theatre of hostilities in North America that resulted in the capitulation of Port-Royal. A new project to conquer Quebec was hatched in England in 1711. Sir Hovenden Walker was appointed commander in chief of a fleet whose mission was to take possession of Canada. After a port visit to Boston to load supplies for a four month expedition, the fleet of nine war ships, 60 transport ships, and two bomb galiots, weighed anchor in Boston with 12,000 men aboard, including 7500 soldiers and a certain number of women accompanying the regiments. The Canadian ship pilot, Jean Paradis, who was taken prisoner at the mouth of the St. Lawrence, was responsible for leading the ships safely up the river despite the bad weather. Thick fog and strong head winds are frequent hazards on the St. Lawrence in August. On September 2, some ships ran afoul of reefs off Egg Island near Sept-Îles leaving some 900 people dead. At the same time an army was stationed on Lake Champlain awaiting news before leaving to join Walker's fleet. When Army Commander Francis Nicholson learned of the catastrophe, he ordered his army to retreat.

When people in Quebec learned in mid-October that for a second time a major attack had been avoided, they rejoiced. The small church on Place Royale, which had been named Notre-Dame-de-la-Victoire (Our Lady of Victory) after Phips's aborted attack, was renamed Notre-Dame-des-Victoires, or Our Lady of Victories.

The war of Spanish succession ended in 1713 with the Treaty of Utrecht, in Holland. Signatories included France, England, Holland, Prussia, Portugal and Savoy. Under the treaty, France ceded Acadia, Newfoundland, and Hudson Bay but kept Cape Breton Island and several islands in the Gulf of St. Lawrence. Moreover, it recognized that the Iroquois would be under British protection. The content of the treaty was a harbinger of the English conquest of New France. For Acadians, it meant the beginning of tribulations that culminated in their being deported from their lands between 1755 and 1762.

In the summer of 1701 representatives of some 40 Aboriginal nations travelled by canoe to Montreal. They came from the entire Great Lakes region, from Baie verte (Green Bay) on the west side of Lake Michigan and Chécago (Chicago) on the southern tip to Baie du tonnerre (Thunder Bay) on the northwest side of Lake Superior. Others came from the upper Mississippi Valley and from what is now northern New York State. When the peace treaty was signed with the French on August 4, 1701, some 1300 representatives of the 40 nations had set up camp in Montreal.

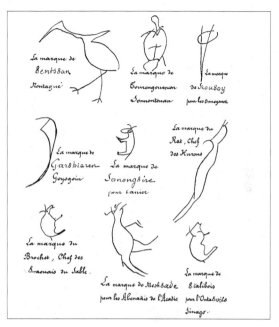

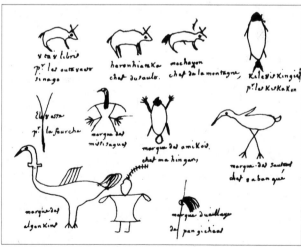

Signatures on the Great Peace or Grand Settlement of Montreal, 1701. These signatures represent the totems symbolizing the names of the leaders of the nations present.

CHAPTER 3

A New People Is Born

By the end of the 17th century, men and women living permanently in Canada had become much different from the people of France, and it was the colonial administrators and visitors who first observed the differences. For Governor Denonville, "The Canadiens are all tall, well built, and solidly set on their legs, accustomed to the necessities of living with little, robust and vigorous, but also strong-willed, light in manner and known for licentiousness. They are good-humoured and lively." In the eyes of the military officer and writer Louis-Armand Lom d'Arce de Lahontan, better known as Baron de Lahontan, "The Canadiens or Creoles [meaning the French born in the colony] are well built, robust, tall, strong, vigorous, hard-working, brave, and indefatigable." Louis-Henri de Baugy, or Chevalier de Baugy, saw the Canadiens in another light. "The men there are very well formed through physical hardship; they travel the woods just like the Savages and some are equally as skilful [...] I would say that the people of this country have a dual nature, stemming both from Savages, big talkers who for the most part know not what they are saying, most of whom claiming also to be gentlemen; as they never agree with one another, one must listen to them talk about each other; it's a fight to shame the other and one simply has to ask a question to find out everything."

Scorn was piled mainly on the youth in the colony as witnessed in this note by Governor Denonville written in 1685. "Young men in Canada are raised so badly that as soon as they know how to carry a gun, their fathers dare not say anything to them. Since they are unaccustomed to work and are poor, they can only rely on the backwoods for resources and are known to leave everything in disarray."

The women in the colony sparked greater interest, especially among the male visitors. For Baron de Lahontan, "the blood in Canada is very fine; women are generally beautiful; brunettes are rare, and many are wise [...] there are many lazy women; they are most keen on luxury and they rival to trap a husband." Baugy was particularly struck by their good moods. "Most of the women have a pleasant demeanour; one should not preach too much to them, I am told, in order to obtain favours from them." Baugy and Lahontan were bachelors and were more impressed by the women than Governor Denonville, who found them lazy and too drawn to luxuries. He believed the long winters to be the cause of the problem. "The winter is long and the people do nothing but keep warm living totally listless lives while the children remain nude; the girls and women remain idle whereas discipline is needed in order to plant hemp and make cloth."

It may have been true that people were somewhat idle in winter, but throughout the summer men and women laboured hard in their fields and tended to their livestock. Townspeople also raised hens and pigs and their vegetable gardens could easily compete with modern gardens. Pierre Boucher described garden fare in 1664 in New France. "All sorts of turnips, rappini, beets, carrots, parsnips, oyster plants, and other root plants grow perfectly and are very large. All types of cabbages grow wonderfully, except for cauliflowers that I have yet to see. As for herbs, sorrel, chards of all types, asparagus, all types of lettuce, chervil, parsley, chicory, burnet, onions, leeks, garlic, chive, hyssop, borage, bugloss, and generally all types of herbs that grow in gardens in France; melons, cucumbers, water melons, and squashes also grow well."

Domestic livestock was imported from France, including cattle, pigs, sheep, and certain types of hens. Fruit trees such as apple and plum trees were also imported. The rivers, lakes, and woods abounded with fish and game. Pierre Boucher savoured moose meat that was "good and light and could never do harm." Other popular game meat included beaver, bear, and porcupine, as well as wild fowl such as goose, partridge, and pigeon. Pigeons were easy game according to Boucher. "They abound and people can kill 40 or 45 with a single shot; that is not what usually happens however; but people will often kill 8, 10 or 12 pigeons; they usually come here in May and leave in September; they can be found throughout this country."

In 17th century Catholic countries, as mentioned earlier, abstinence from eating meat was the rule for 140 days a year. In New France beavers were found everywhere and one obvious question arose. Was the beaver an animal or a fish? If it belonged to the fish family, it could be served throughout the year. Bishop François de Laval submitted this important question to theologians at the Sorbonne and to doctors at Paris's Hôtel-Dieu hospital. The experts earnestly discussed the issue at length and consulted other illustrious scientists and came down with the conclusion that the beaver was a fish because of its tail. The decision brought joy to the colony.

The colony imported the foodstuffs it did not produce, including salt, pepper, nutmeg, cloves, brown and white sugar, olive oil, and lemon peels. By the end of the 17th century, people were producing maple sugar that sometimes replaced cane sugar. They tended nonetheless to prefer the wine and spirits from France, although some brave souls attempted to make wine with local grapes. Pierre Boucher scoffed at the "heavy red wine that leaves stains."

Many travellers were very impressed by the hospitality of the Canadians who readily opened their doors and set their tables for foreign guests. Curiosity might partially explain their hospitality. People danced and ate well in winter, particularly between Christmas and Mardi Gras. Religious leaders railed against "mixed" dancing that had both sexes doing quadrilles and minuets together. They frowned even more upon the charivari, which had been banned throughout the Catholic world in the 16th century under penalty of excommunication. In New France charivaris became popular in the 1680s. People would make a hullabaloo to protest a wedding or widowhood that was too brief, or to oppose marriage of a bride and a groom who were too far apart in age. Very often the only way to stop a charivari was to pay off its organizers. Those who organized charivaris were threatened with excommunication in 1683, as were the parents of young people or the servant masters who allowed them to carry on the way they did.

Whereas the moral fibre of the colony raised eyebrows in some circles, maintaining good health was a serious challenge. Scurvy ravaged New France in the early years but ebbed as people began eating fresh unsalted meat and vegetables. Pierre Boucher even idealized the climate, especially in the winter. "The air is extremely healthy at all times but above all in the winter." Child mortality nonetheless was a scourge with hundreds of children dying. Epidemics also regularly plagued the inhabitants. The first typhus epidemic swept through in 1659 and yet another hit the colony in 1665 immediately after the ships carrying the Carignan-Salières regiment had arrived. On a single ship, quite ironically named

La Justice, 100 soldiers succumbed. Typhus struck again in 1685 killing approximately a hundred inhabitants and two years later smallpox swept through leaving in its wake another 500 Canadians dead. Then in the winter of 1702-03, thirteen percent of the population of Quebec City, or approximately 260 people, were wiped out by still another smallpox epidemic. These figures show that Boucher's observations about the healthy climate were off the mark to say the least.

The colony had five hospitals with Quebec and Montréal both boasting a Hôtel-Dieu hospital. Early in the 1690s both cities could also rely on general hospitals for the poor, the beggars, and the able-bodied and disabled inhabitants. When these people were sick they were treated at the Hôtel-Dieu. In Trois-Rivières, Monsignor Saint-Vallier requested that the Ursuline Sisters found a hospital. "There will be six beds with clean straw mattresses covered with serge or woven sheets," wrote Sister Thérèse Germain. "Near each bed there is a chair and a chiffonier. Running water and sewers are still unknown in Trois-Rivières: well water is brought for the patients to drink and wash, and, of course, under each bed can be found another essential accessory."

The Ursuline Sisters educated the girls in Trois-Rivières and Quebec, while the Sisters of the Congregation of Notre-Dame opened schools in several parishes in Montreal. The Jesuit College was still the only institution providing classical education. The Sulpicians in Montreal founded a school for boys. A certain number of teachers also travelled from town to town and provided a summary education to those prepared to pay. Young men wishing to become priests lived at the Séminaire de Québec and received their instruction from Jesuits.

The clergy maintained a constant surveillance over those responsible for education, as they did in other walks of life. The majority of the population were devout Catholics partly because Protestantism was forbidden. People rarely skipped religious services on Sundays and feast days. In addition to the 52 Sundays in the calendar, there were 37 compulsory feast days. Work was forbidden on those days. At times the civil authorities fined people who did not honour the "Lord's day."

In some ways the Canadians were still French while in others they had developed very differently. The Jesuit François-Xavier de Charlevoix related his observations about the "Creoles of Canada" in 1720. "They debate the past, and surmise the future; science and fine arts are contemplated, and conversation is lively. The Canadians, that is the Creoles of Canada, exude a nascent air of liberty which renders them very pleasant in the business of life. Nowhere else does one speak our language more purely. No accent can be detected here." A decade later, Pierre-Olivier Thoulier d'Olivet, a member of the Académie française, added that "An opera can be sent to Canada and it will be sung at Quebec with every note and tone being as fine as in Paris; however if a sentence from a conversation is sent to Bordeaux or Montpellier the syllables will not be pronounced as they would in Paris."

The language spoken by the Canadians grew richer as new words and expressions were added to deal with their different conditions. Shortly before the Conquest, the French army officer Jean-Baptiste d'Aleyrac, who fought in the battle of the Plains of Abraham, had rubbed shoulders long enough with the Canadians to observe the language they spoke. "There is no patois in this country. All the Canadians speak French just as we do." He added that they had borrowed many words from mariners and replaced words used elsewhere. Some examples were "amarrer" meaning to moor or make fast instead of "attacher," or "haler" meaning to haul in or tow instead of "tirer." New words observed included "tuque" which had replaced the term "bonnet de laine," a very popular and useful piece of winter clothing. Many of the words and expressions and their derivatives observed by d'Aleyrac in the mid-17th century are still used today throughout Quebec.

A Canadien heads off to war in the winter. The people had adapted rapidly to the climate of the country and to the ways of the original inhabitants.

The horse-drawn carriage or calèche was widely used to travel between Montreal and Quebec City. As of 1749 it was forbidden to park one's calèche in the streets of Montreal.

CHAPTER 4

A Conquest Foretold

The Treaty of Utrecht amputated a large portion of New France's territory which meant that the time had come to fortify the colony so that it could resist over the long term against the very many in New England who wanted to defeat New France once and for all. The Acadians were pressured to emigrate to other parts of New France, but few went along. Efforts were also made to convince the Canadians that the construction of a fortress at Louisburg on Cape Breton Island, renamed Isle Royale, represented an efficient safeguard against attacks by the English. Over time it became obvious however that Cape Breton, sometimes erroneously called "America's Gibraltar," had nowhere near the defence capacity provided by the real Gibraltar. The Governor of New France, Charles de Beauharnois de la Boische, was fully aware of its deficiencies when he wrote that "The entire English army could reach Quebec and nobody on Isle Royale would know; what's more, even if they knew, what could they do?"

Quebec and Montreal had to be fortified. Two new redoubts were built in Quebec, La Royale and La Dauphine. Construction had begun by 1720 and although it was nowhere near being completed people still felt that the city could be defended. The Jesuit historian Charlevoix noted that "Quebec is not fortified in the regular fashion, but work has been underway for a long time to make it a good place. This city is not easy to take in its natural state. The port is sided with two ramparts that during high tide are almost at water level, meaning that they rise 25 feet above the ground, since the equinox tide reaches that high. Just above the right rampart, another half rampart is anchored in the rock, and above that, beside the fort's gallery, there is a battery of 25 cannons. A small square fort known as the Citadelle is still higher and the paths leading from one fortification to another are extremely steep." More defensive works had been built along the Saint-Charles River and in the area of Cap aux Diamants.

Quebec could expect threats to come mainly from enemy ships that would attack as they arrived from the mouth of the St. Lawrence. Montreal on the other hand had to prepare for attackers who would travel down the Richelieu River, the most commonly used route, to its mouth on the St. Lawrence just downstream from Montreal. It was therefore decided to reinforce the city by replacing the cedar pile wall with a stone wall. Quebec's fortifications were being financed by the King's Treasury, but Montrealers learned to their chagrin that they and those under the Montreal administration would have to contribute through forced work or a kind of tax. These measures upset many in the city to the point that, in summer 1717, those living in the village of Longueuil just across the river protested by refusing to work. Some were arrested and thrown in jail for months.

Montreal's fortifications were only completed towards the end of the 1730s but the result was amazing. Historian Jean-Claude Robert observed that "the fort had a circumference of 3500 metres and comprised 14 defensive walls, namely 13 ramparts linked to each other by curtain walls, in addition to the citadel. The walls were about six metres high and had gun ports at approximately every two metres. The walls were not as thick on the river side as on the inland side, the reason being that with the currents and shoals in the port an attack from the river was unlikely and, in any case, the slow man-oeuvring of the ships would make them relatively easy targets for gunners in Montreal. On the inland side, the engineer had called for a ditch and downward slope or glacis stretching for more than 60 meters from the wall. In all the walls had 16 gates and posterns, including 10 leading to the St. Lawrence. The gates were wide enough for carts to be used, while the posterns were for pedestrians and soldiers."

New forts were also built in the Lake Champlain area and in the Pays-d'en-Haut, which included the upper Great Lakes, and on strategic points in the Hudson Bay and Mississippi watersheds. The names given to those forts and the surround-ing rivers, lakes, and mountains, very often French renditions of Aboriginal names, have remained to this day. In some places the French and English forts, serving both fur trade and defence purposes, stood face to face. The never-ending need to find new sources of fur supplies as well as the dream of a route to China pushed Pierre Gaultier de Varennes et de La Vérendrye to set out to explore the West. Earnings from the fur trade and not the King's Treasury made his long march to the Rocky Mountains possible. On his way he estab-lished many new forts but he and his men encountered oppos-ition from some Aboriginal nations allied with the Sioux. A number of traders were massacred in 1736 including La Vérendrye's eldest son. The trip across the continent would never have been successful had the Canadians not enjoyed the help and cooperation of Aboriginal nations all along the way. Two years later the Mandans of the Upper Missouri River told La Vérendrye about a huge body of water where the other side could not be seen and where "the water is bad to drink." Convinced that the body of water was the Vermeille Sea leading to China, La Vérendrye instructed his son Louis-

Joseph to go and explore the area south of the forty-ninth parallel. On January 1, 1743 Louis-Joseph came within sight of huge mountains and was undoubtedly the first European to see the Rocky Mountains.

During the first half of the 18th century, the economy of New France no longer depended exclusively on furs. Governors and intendants sought to find out if there were any mines to exploit. The Aboriginal people had spoken about a copper mine on the south side of Lake Superior on what is now known as the Keenawa Peninsula. Ore from that mine was sent to France to be assayed and reports indicated that it was 90 percent pure. Experts at the Paris Mint were astonished and convinced that the "piece of copper sent to France was not in its natural state and that it had already been smelted." These copper deposits however would not be developed commercially until the 1840s.

The lead mine discovered in Baie-Saint-Paul on the north shore of the St. Lawrence downstream from Quebec, however, failed to impress Swedish-Finnish scientist Pehr Kalm during his trip in 1749. "It appears clearly that it is not worth extracting the ore. On the one hand, the veins are very narrow and tightly trapped and much work would be required to break the hard granite around it; on the other, this ore is poor and would far from cover the cost, especially because of the cost of manpower in this area." The colony's lack of any really skilled miners also discouraged anybody who might have wished to operate the mine.

The iron mines in the vicinity of Trois-Rivières were another story. Under Jean Talon several barrels of iron ore had already been shipped to France to determine whether it was wise to build an ironworks there. That shipment met with a positive response and new iron ore deposits were found in the Cap-de-la-Madeleine and Champlain areas in 1672 shortly after Frontenac arrived. Before operations could begin, however, the King's Minister Colbert had to approve them, which he failed to do. His successor Maurepas finally replied in the negative in 1717. "HRH (His Royal Highness) does not consider it appropriate to work the iron mines. France has enough iron to supply all of Canada." Mercantilism still held sway and that meant that production in the colonies could not compete with produce from the mother country.

The Montreal merchant François Poulin de Francheville nonetheless obtained a licence from the government of Trois-Rivières in 1730 to mine the iron ore. French authorities had changed their minds mainly because the merchant had undertaken to finance and build the ironworks himself in return for certain privileges. Work was delayed owing both to funding problems and to recruitment of skilled workers and, as a result, the blast furnace was only fired up officially eight years later on August 20, 1738. Serious financial problems continued to plague the undertaking. Intendant Gilles Hocquart managed to avoid a total shut-down by subsidizing it and making it a state-owned company. Poor administration and hostile relations between the ironworks master and workers caused the ironworks to go bankrupt. Tough times would continue for the Forges du Saint-Maurice, as the ironworks were known. The Governor of Trois-Rivières, Pierre-François Rigaud de Vaudreuil, wrote in 1749 that "the cost was extraordinary. The ironworks are badly managed. Fires eat up the wood, the wood is poorly cut, and the horned animals that are left chew up and eliminate the wood that would grow and that could be used to make charcoal. There are several masters. None is a skilled selfless manager upon whom the workers and the inspectors can count."

The Saint-Maurice ironworks was the biggest industry in the colony, employing several hundred workers. It manufactured ploughshares, pots, pans, stove tops, cannonballs, cannons, and more. Pehr Kalm was particularly impressed. "It is the only one in Canada. [...] There are several buildings and two drop hammers, each in its own building; in each building there is a large hammer as well as another smaller one; the bellows are made of wood and all the rest is like it is at home in Sweden. The blast furnace is located right near the drop hammers and is also built as it is at home."

Logging for shipbuilding expanded in the first decades of the 18th century. Pine and spruce timber was required for the masts, birch was needed for the keels, hemlock for the gunwales, and ash for the framework. Several shipyards sprung up in and around Quebec, at the Anse-des-Mères, to the west of Cul-du-Sac, and on the banks of the Saint-Charles River. Many warships were produced but often aid from His Majesty was required for the shipyards to survive. Without the King's support the industry might never have existed. According to historian Jacques Mathieu, "the shipbuilding industry in Quebec City was in fact an extension of the mother country by the capital used and its the overall purpose, as well as by the methods used and the management of manpower, in short, by its very nature. High-level decisions were always made in France. They were made for, and to the benefit of, the mother country, not the colony. The minister Maurepas demanded that the intendant comply with a type of construction that did not match forestry resources in New France. French construction methods were not successfully adapted to conditions in Canada either. Skilled workers brought over from France did not encourage the Canadians to abandon their voluntary isolation [...] Ambitions were too great for industrial development of New France in the middle of the 18th century."

Manpower shortages or lack of know-how and funding caused problems in most areas of economic activity. As elsewhere, get rich quick schemes were launched and ended up backfiring. When the Jesuit Joseph-François Lafitau learned from another missionary in Asia that the Chinese were particularly keen on ginseng, a plant known for its aphrodisiac properties, he wrote to the Regent about it in 1718. The Chinese in fact imported large quantities of ginseng from Korea and Lafitau was convinced that the plant grew in the St. Lawrence Valley. What's more, the Iroquois were already using the plant because it had "the virtue of making women fertile." People in New France rushed to find the plant and that drove prices up rapidly, reaching a summit 25 times higher than the original price. In 1751 alone ginseng shipments to France were enormous. Greed however led people to defy the normal rules for picking and drying the plant. The desired aphrodisiac properties of ginseng were obtained by picking it in September and carefully drying it by turning it over several times a day. Ginseng producers in Canada started picking it in May and drying it in ovens so as to make money quickly. The product lost its aphrodisiac powers and the Chinese stopped purchasing ginseng from Canada. Thus, what might have become a highly lucrative industry was almost dead in 1752. That year the engineer Louis Franquet foresaw the approaching collapse. "All the inhabitants, including the Savages, have dropped everything to produce ginseng. It is wild these days, but unfortunately nobody waits until the plant is ripe and as a result, quality suffers. They will put an end to a product that could have been among greatest sources of wealth for this country."

Fisheries fortunately continued to thrive, particularly because fish were still highly valued. When Acadia and Newfoundland were lost to England, the fishery flourished on the Gaspé Peninsula. "The role of dry cod on the Gaspé Peninsula," wrote historian David Lee, "clearly contributed to making a society quite different from the one in Canada where means of subsistence were much more diversified. It appears that the inhabitants of Pabos [on the south shore of the Gaspé Peninsula] are in much better health than elsewhere in New France, indicating a higher standard of living." In the Rivière-Ouelle area, down river from Quebec City, hunting for porpoises for oil and leather was a major activity. People also hunted seals and used seal hides for plough handles.

In times of peace most sectors of the economy prospered more than in wartime. But in mid-March 1744 a new war broke out between France and England over succession to the emperor of Austria who had died. Just over a year later, after a 47-day siege, the fort of Louisburg fell. People in Quebec focussed on getting the fort back because they felt threatened and vulnerable. In the eyes of Gaspard-Joseph Chausse-gros de Léry "the loss of Louisburg concerned the entire navy and opened the door for the English to take over this colony. [...] The whole country hopes that the King will not abandon Louisburg to the English." Attempts to reconquer that fort met with failure.

Since the people living along the St. Lawrence Valley feared invasion, a coast guard network was established between Lévis, across from Quebec City, and Rimouski, on the lower south shore of the St. Lawrence. In an aim to terrorize the enemy, allied Aboriginal nations raided English settlements and brought back scalps as trophies. Their actions provoked the ire of New England authorities who considered the practice to be barbaric, but in fact both sides regularly bought scalps taken from their enemies.

The King's minister Maurepas stated that if the colony wanted to be fortified its inhabitants would have to foot the cost. France and England fortunately signed a peace treaty however at Aix-la-Chapelle on October 28, 1748. The treaty restored the pre-war situation, with Louisburg being returned to France. It also gave rise to new expression "bête comme la paix" (stupid as the peace).

Peace was widely perceived to be shaky and, to add to fears in Canada, English authorities in London and New England made no bones about their desire to settle the question of New France once and for all.

As both sides scrambled to build new forts and reinforce existing settlements, Acadia became a hot spot. The vast majority of Acadians were opposed to swearing unconditional allegiance to England because they did not wish to take up arms for their new mother country. As a result they became foreigners on lands they had cleared and settled many decades earlier and in the eyes of the English Crown they represented a permanent threat to the English minority that now lived in Acadia. Most of all, the new English settlers in the Halifax area coveted the Acadians' land. The English decided to deport them in 1755, primarily to New England, and despite the gravity of the operation, French authorities, be it in Paris or Quebec, showed little opposition. Worse yet, when the St. Lawrence Valley was hit with a serious famine in 1757, some people urged that the borders be closed to Acadians seeking refuge in French lands. The Acadians were accused of bringing death with them since many were sick and on the verge of starvation.

The Seven Years' War only began officially in 1756, but war had already been raging in North America for two years. People in the English colonies saw the "reduction of Canada" as a necessity. Different names are used to qualify that war depending on which side people or their ancestors were on. For Europeans and English-speaking Canadians it is known as the "Seven Years' War," for the inhabitants of New France, now Quebec, it is known as the "Guerre de la conquête" or "War of Conquest;" and for the people of New England, and eventually all of the United States, it is known as the "French and Indian War." Winston Churchill would later call it the "First World War."

The combined Canadian and Aboriginal troops were victorious when the first battles broke out in the Ohio River Valley in July 1754. A relatively minor incident at Fort Necessity has since been recognized as the spark that led to the ultimate defeat of the French in North America and even to the American Revolution. People in Virginia saw the Ohio and Monongahela rivers as the natural extension of their colony and were intent on settling there. The French were in the process of building forts in the area to reaffirm their control. A young officer by the name of George Washington was sent to build a fort near the French Fort Duquesne, where Pittsburgh is now located. On May 18, 1754, with about 100 men, Washington encountered Jumonville and 34 men who had orders to expel the Virginians from the area. Washington's men opened fire and killed Jumonville and nine men. What was a "border incident" for the Virginians became a casus belli for the French and Canadians. Jumonville's brother Coulon de Villiers was sent to avenge the "assassination." With 500 men, he attacked Fort Necessity and defeated Washington and his troops, most of whom were drunk. Montreal historian Guy Frégault pointed out that although it was a minor clash, that battle in the Ohio River Valley "was part of a drama whose final scene would be played out at the foot of the walls of Montreal on September 8, 1760. The taking over of Fort Necessity was not the cause of the War of Conquest, but it marked the beginning of its main phase." Another battle on the Monongahela with similar stakes in 1755 resulted in another victory for the French and Aboriginal troops.

The war also provided the occasion for two different military strategies to clash, conventional European methods versus tactics used by the Canadians and their allies and by some New Englanders. For regular soldiers, the army had to march to drumbeat over level land in an orderly fashion and wait for orders to fire. The militias and their Aboriginal allies on the other hand made the most of the terrain, hiding behind trees and in ravines and shooting when ready. One English officer even described war tactics of the North American as murder.

All able-bodied Canadians between 16 and 60 had been drafted into militias since 1669 and were placed under the orders of a captain who drilled them in the use of weapons. When conscripted, they had to choose between showing up as ordered or facing the death penalty. What's more, each had to supply his own food and clothing. Since they were often called up during summer, they had to abandon their crops, which led many to desert. Several regular army officers nonetheless had nothing but praise for the militiamen. "The Canadians can be considered to be light troops," wrote Ensign Louis-Guillaume de Pascarau du Plessis to his wife. "They go to war as the Savages do, preferring to ambush and surprise the enemy than to attack in the wide open. They are robust and accustomed from a very young age to travel in the woods and can put up with the fatigue that comes with hunting. The English who are not as alert nor as brave are always caught off guard because they never train in the woods like our Canadians do, and this will always give us superiority since the battles must be fought in the woods which cover the entire country; unless of course we were to stay in the forts as the English do."

Even before France and England declared war, France appointed Marquis Louis-Joseph de Montcalm commander

of French troops in North America with the position of
major-general or "maréchal de camp." The question remained
as to who held supreme authority, the Governor General
François-Pierre de Rigaud de Vaudreuil-Cavagnial, the first
Canadian-born man to hold the position, or Montcalm? King
Louis XV made it clear when he declared, "In a word, it is up
to the Governor General to settle everything and order all
military operations. The Sieur marquis de Montcalm shall be
held to execute his orders. He will nonetheless be able to make
representations that he judges suitable regarding projects he
has been ordered to execute. Should the Governor General
believe he has reason not to defer to him or to continue as
planned, the Sieur marquis de Montcalm shall comply post-
haste and in good will." The French general was loath to obey
orders from a Canadian.

Montcalm spurned the presence of Aboriginal troops
among the Canadian militias and along side regular French
troops, claiming that they were hard to control. In his diary
entry for October 20, 1756 he wrote that "they get excited,
deliberate slowly among themselves, and they want to go and
attack together and on the same side because they like large
battalions. From the time they resolve to act until they act,
much time goes by; one nation will stop the march and then
another nation will do the same. They all need time to get
drunk and the amounts they imbibe are enormous. They
finally go to battle but once they have struck, even if they have
only taken one scalp or one prisoner, they return and then go
home to their villages. Therefore, the army has been without
Savages for a long time. For the individual, that is better, but
war operations have suffered because they are nonetheless a
necessary evil. It would be better to have a set number of these
mosquitoes at a particular time and who can be replaced by
others in such a manner as to always have some." French

officers begrudgingly admitted nonetheless that Aboriginal troops were required in order to conduct war properly.

Intendant François Bigot and his men were instructed to find the wherewithal to feed the army. The inhabitants were obliged to sell their livestock and agricultural produce at prices set by the intendant, who in turn sold them to the King at a comfortable, if not excessive, profit. The cost of living shot up and scarcity became a scourge. On September 14, 1757, after famine had struck the colony, Montcalm described the situation in his diary: "A soldier's daily ration will be half a pound of bread and a quarter pound of peas; every eight days, six pounds of fresh beef and two pounds of cod. We fear that we will be unable to sustain these rations and, in time, will be obliged to serve horsemeat. No lard will be given now since there must be no shortage; moreover cattle are at their best and yield the most at this time of year."

People began to protest and demonstrate believing that the famine was artificial and that the "Bigot gang" was simply hoarding in the hope of jacking prices up even higher. Beef may well have become scarce but horses were in abundance throughout the colony. Bigot estimated that the colony had about 3000 horses and so civil and military authorities set out to convince the soldiers and the general population to eat horse meat. Vaudreuil, Bigot, Montcalm, and Brigadier François-Gaston de Lévis tried setting an example by preparing a meal based entirely on horse meat. It featured "small horsemeat pies à l'espagnole; horse à la mode; horse scallops; horse on a skewer with a thick pepper sauce; horse hoofs au gratin; horse tongue miroton; frigousse horse stew; smoked horse tongue and horse cakes, like hare cakes." They soon learned that you can put horse meat on the table, but you cannot make the soldiers and the people eat it. Lévis went as far as threatening to hang any man who refused a plate of horse meat, but the Canadians reacted even more stubbornly, refusing to be forced to eat their best friend! As a result, famine continued to plague Quebec and Montreal relentlessly. The following year, women demonstrated for bread, which was increasingly expensive and whose quality was constantly degenerating.

The English began to gain the upper hand on the battlefields partly because Prime Minister William Pitt of England believed that war between England and France would be won in America. New England could count on 33,000 men comprising 12,000 soldiers and 21,000 militiamen. The King of France on the other hand believed that the victor would be determined in Europe and, as a result, the colony was left with a mere 6800 regular soldiers and a few thousand militiamen. England's Thirteen Colonies in America at this point were 20 times more populated than France's colonies.

At the beginning of the war each side won some battles and lost others, but winds began to change in 1758. Montcalm commanded his last great battle at Carillon, now known as Ticonderoga, in New York State, and that battle has gone down in history in Quebec. A few days later, however, James Wolfe, who had been appointed temporarily Brigadier General in America, led a land attack on Louisburg and took the fort. His only desire then was to sail up the St. Lawrence Valley and reduce the Canadians for good. He wrote to General Jeffrey Amherst on August 8: "I cannot look coolly upon the bloody inroads of those hell-hounds the Canadians; and if nothing further is to be done, I must desire leave to quit the army." In the meantime, Wolfe was instructed to destroy French settlements on the Gaspé Peninsula. He later described that campaign: "We have done a great deal of mischief,— spread the terror of His Majesty's arms through the whole gulf; but have added nothing to the reputation of them."

Somewhat ironically Wolfe was accompanied by many Scottish Highlanders whom he professed to hate and whom he had fought and defeated a mere 13 years earlier, notably at the bloody battle of Culloden, near Inverness in Scotland. Wolfe was a young aide-de-camp to a general reporting to the commander, the Duke of Cumberland, who was later dubbed the "butcher of Culloden" because of the brutal massacre that occurred. In a letter about the Highlanders that he managed to recruit, Wolfe wrote that "They are hardy, intrepid, accustomed to a rough country, and no great mischief if they fall."

Early in 1759 Officer Louis-Antoine de Bougainville travelled to France to request reinforcements from the Minister of Marine, Nicolas-René Berryer. The rebuff was brutal but enlightening as to how France perceived its colony. "With the house on fire we are not going to save the stables." Bougainville in turn waxed ironic: "I can thus only obtain for the stables but 400 recruits and a small amount of ammunition." As Montcalm wished, the army pulled back around Quebec. The animosity that poisoned his relationship with Governor Vaudreuil had heightened when Montcalm was promoted Lieutenant General on October 20, 1758, thereby making him Governor Vaudreuil's superior.

The people in the capital of New France knew that Quebec was the next target of English attacks. The enemy fleet under the command of Admiral Charles Saunders was quite literally an armada, counting 29 large navy ships, 12 frigates and corvettes, 2 galiots with bombs, 80 cargo ships, and between 50 and 60 small craft or schooners. In all, the fleet had some 1900 cannon as well as 8500 troops under Wolfe's command and 13,500 seamen and crew. With all the other passengers included, a total of 30,000 people arrived in reinforcement. Montcalm's forces pale in comparison: 15,000 men including regular soldiers, troops from the Marine, and militiamen. He could also count upon about a thousand Aboriginal troops.

Most of the women and children living on the south shore of the St. Lawrence took refuge inland, while the Île d'Orléans just downstream from Quebec was deserted by the majority of its inhabitants. What's more, the English army set up camp on the island on June 27. Wolfe posted instructions to the inhabitants that set the tone for his future actions. He informed the inhabitants in French that they would be allowed to come to their families and their homes; he promised "to protect them" and assured them that "they need not fear being molested in any way, that they could enjoy the use of their property and follow their cult and religious rites; in a word, while war raged, they could enjoy the sweetness of peace, on the condition that they undertake not to take sides directly or indirectly in a dispute that only concerned the two crowns. On the other hand, should some displaced stubbornness or imprudent and useless value lead them to take up arms, they shall expect to suffer whatever cruelties that war can inflict upon them. It is easy to understand to what excesses the furor of a frantic soldier might take him; only our orders can stop that and it is up to the Canadians, through their conduct, to obtain this advantage for themselves." Two days later the same instructions were posted on the church at Beaumont on the south shore.

English troops took position on the Pointe-Lévy training their cannons on Quebec, and for the first time since war had broken out Quebec closed the city gates on June 30. A few days later, the English established another beachhead, but this time on the north shore of the St. Lawrence on the left bank of the Montmorency River downstream from Quebec. Montcalm was thus convinced the English would attack Quebec from Beauport to the north east of the capital, so he set up camp there.

The English started bombing Quebec on July 12 in the evening destroying or razing by fire nearly 250 houses in less than a week. Some people had managed to evacuate the city before the bombing campaign began. Bombing continued almost every night until September 13. Four hundred English grenadiers landed at the tiny village of Pointe-aux-Trembles 30 kilometres upstream and captured 200 women and children, including some wealthy ladies who had fled the bombing in Quebec. Wolfe brought them back and freed them at Anse au Foulon where it was observed that they took a path that enabled them to climb up to the Plains of Abraham with ease. The English general undoubtedly had aboard the ship the spy Robert Stobo, a Scot who had escaped from Quebec early in May. Since Stobo had lived in Quebec unfettered after promising not to escape, he had undoubtedly heard of the path up to the Plains. Wolfe carefully digested this intelligence.

Despite all General Wolfe's threats, hundreds of Canadians constantly harassed enemy camps killing and scalping soldiers that they caught. Wolfe prohibited scalping "except when the enemies are Indians or Canadians dressed like Indians." When the Canadians refused neutrality, Wolfe ordered the destruction of the entire region from the Chaudière River near Lévis to Kamouraska some 160 kilometres east of Quebec on the south shore of the St. Lawrence. On July 25 he posted a proclamation on the door of the Saint-Henri de Lauzon Church. In French Wolfe informed the inhabitants that "His Excellence was upset by the lack of attention they had paid to his proclamation posted on June 27; he thus resolved to ignore the feelings of humanity that had led him to relieve people who were blinded in their own misery. By their conduct, the Canadiens showed that they were unworthy of the advantageous offers he had made to them. For that reason, he ordered the commander of his light brigades and other officers to advance through the country and to capture and bring back the inhabitants and their live-stock and to destroy and overturn everything that they deemed necessary."

George Scott and the 1600 men in his command destroyed homes and fields. In his September 19 report Scott wrote that they had marched a distance of some 52 miles and along the way had burned 998 good buildings, 2 sloops, 2 schooners, 10 longboats, several barges, and small craft. He added that they had captured 15 prisoners (including six women and five children) and killed five people from among the enemy. One of Scott's regular soldiers died, while there were two casualties and four wounded among the Rangers.

The two armies rarely engaged in major battles. On July 31 Wolfe attempted to land at the Montmorency River, but his men were beaten back and they suffered many casualties. The English army's inertia can partly be explained by Wolfe's poor health. In a letter on August 31 to his mother—Wolfe was a bachelor—he described the situation as follows: "My antagonist has wisely shut himself up in inaccessible entrenchments, so that I cant get at him without spilling a torrent of blood, and that perhaps to little purpose. The Marquis de Montcalm is at the head of a great number of bad soldiers, and I am at the head of a small number of good ones, that wish for nothing so much as to fight him—but the wary old fellow avoids an action doubtful of the behaviour of his army. People must be of the profession to understand the disadvantages and difficulties we labour under arising from the uncommon natural strength of the country."

The French expected the attack to come from Beauport downstream and thus had only set up one guard post on the Plains of Abraham, but Wolfe had already decided some time earlier that the landing would take place at Anse au Foulon, later to be known as Wolfe's Cove and in military circles as Wolfe's stronghold. He informed Brigadiers General George Townshend and Robert Monckton, who had directed the deportation of Acadians in 1755, and Admiral Saunders of his plans on September 10. Moreover he stingingly retorted to generals who doubted the potential of the landing spot. "It is my duty to attack the French army. To the best of my knowledge and abilities, I have fixed upon this spot, where we can act with the most force and are most likely to succeed. If I am mistaken I am sorry for it and must be answerable to his Majesty and the public for the consequences."

English troops landed during the night on September 13 and easily had seized the guard post before the alert sounded in Quebec at 5:30 in the morning. The soldiers took an hour and a quarter to leave their camp at Beauport where they had been expecting the attack all night. Shortly before 10 o'clock, the armies stood face to face. On the English side the soldiers waited in combat lines for orders to fire while on the French side, the Canadians and their Aboriginal allies started shooting at the enemy, but Montcalm was hesitant. He nonetheless told an assistant: "We cannot avoid combat. The enemy is dug in; he already has two pieces of cannon. If we give him the time to establish himself, we'll never be able to attack him with the few troops we have. Is it possible that Bougainville doesn't know this?"

The battle lasted no more than half an hour. The French troops along with the Canadian and Aboriginal militiamen were routed. Wolfe died on the battlefield while Montcalm was mortally wounded and died the following night never to hear the reproaches levelled at him for not waiting for reinforcements that would have allowed him to attack Wolfe on two fronts. Wolfe was not beyond reproach either, having positioned his men in a manner that made retreat impossible.

Quebec historian Guy Frégault suggests that September 13 should be known as the "Day of Mistakes." "Wolfe's pale victory resulted from the fact that Montcalm made more mistakes than he."

Wealthy people in Quebec sneered at the idea of resisting and preferred capitulation, which took place on September 18. All was not lost, however, as Bougainville pointed out. "The English still only control the walls, but the colony still belongs to the King." The French army retreated to Pointe-aux-Trembles 30 kilometres upriver and then to the right bank of the Jacques-Cartier River a few kilometres farther. Troops skirmished during the winter but avoided any major clashes. With Montcalm's death, Lévis had taken command and he insisted that Quebec had to be recaptured before the ice broke in the spring and made navigation possible. He marched on Quebec and resumed hostilities at Sainte-Foy on April 28, 1760. This time the French troops were victorious and Major General James Murray, the occupying Governor of Quebec, had to retreat with his troops to within the walls of Quebec while Lévis laid siege to Quebec, camping just outside the fortifications. That proved to be a Pyrrhic victory when on May 9 a ship flying the flag of England arrived at Quebec followed six days later by three warships that anchored right in front of the city. At that point, the French army pulled back to Montreal.

Three armies marched on Montreal in the summer of 1760 and made resistance appear so futile that Governor Vaudreuil decided to capitulate. During capitulation negotiations, the victorious English denied the honours of war to the defeated army. Shuddering at the idea of handing over his colours, Lévis ordered that they be burned on Île Sainte-Hélène across from the city of Montreal. Quebec City fell on September 18, 1759 and year later, on September 8, the whole of New France capitulated. An article in the capitulation agreement concerned the militias. "They will return to their homes without being molested on any pretence, on account of their having borne arms." The inhabitants were granted the right to freely practise their religion but tithing by priests was to "depend on the King's will." Article 32 stipulated that "the communities of Nuns shall be preserved in their constitutions and privileges; they shall continue to observe their rules, they shall be exempted from lodging any military; and it shall be forbid to molest them in their religious exercises, or to enter their nonasteries: safe-guards shall even be given them, if they desire them." The male religious orders had to wait for the King of England to express his will. He chose to disband them.

People wishing to return to France received authorization to do so. Neither the Canadians nor the French were to be deported, but the Acadians who had sought refuge in New France were let off not so easily. "It is up to the King to dispose of his former subjects; in the meantime, they would enjoy the same privileges as the Canadiens." The latter did not receive the assurance that they could keep French law nor have the right to remain neutral should another war break out. As for the "negro and pawnee" slaves... they were to remain slaves!

All was not over yet since peace negotiations and the peace treaty could alter the picture. Hope thus remained alive in the hearts of some.

When it was dark and foggy, English troops landed at the Anse au Foulon or Wolfe's Cove at the foot of a cliff and climbed up to the Plains of Abraham on the night of September 12-13, 1759.

The much-storied church Notre-Dame-des-Victoires was left in ruins after the battle for Quebec.

contenües dans le dit Traité, moyennant Son

Les presens Articles separés auront la même Force, que s'ils etoient inserés dans le Traité.

En Foy de quoi nous soussignés Ambassadeurs Extraordinaires et Ministres Plenipotentiaires de Leurs Majestes Britannique, Tres Chretienne, et Catholique, avons Signé les presens Articles separés, et y avons fait apposer le Cachet de Nos Armes.

Fait à Paris le Dix de Fevrier Mil sept cent soixante et trois.

The Treaty of Paris signed on February 10, 1763 by Louis XV, King of France, George III, King of England, Charles III, King of Spain, and Joseph I, King of Portugal, put an end to the Seven Years' War.

Interestingly, the treaty that opened the St. Lawrence Valley to English colonization was drafted in French only!

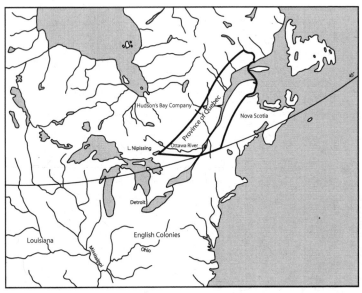

New France had disappeared and the British created a new colony in 1763, the Province of Quebec.

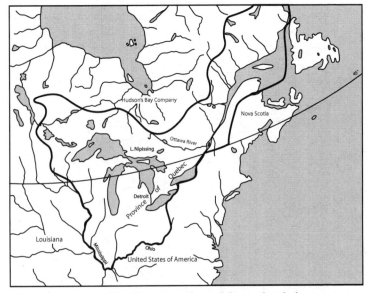

In 1774 the Province of Quebec was made much larger than before.

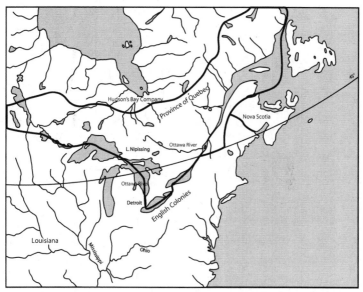

With the independence of the United States in 1783, the Province of Quebec was granted new boundaries stretching much farther west.

CHAPTER 5

Former Enemies Forced to Live Together

Faced with the challenge of becoming familiar with the land, army engineers from the conquering English army visited the parishes administered by Montreal and established contact with militia captains. The French civil authorities and senior army personnel had left the colony and the English military had taken over, thereby marking the beginning of the "military regime." The people were forced to hand over their guns but some managed to retrieve them soon after for hunting.

The conquest made the Canadians "new subjects" of the King of England, as opposed to the English who were the "old subjects" or "natural born subjects." To foster understanding, General Jeffrey Amherst posted the following decree in French on September 22, 1760: "As the troops have been explicitly ordered to live with the inhabitants in harmony and understanding, we recommend that the inhabitants receive the troops and treat them as brothers and fellow citizens. The inhabitants are also ordered to listen to and obey all orders from their governors and from those to whom our right has been conferred; and as long as the inhabitants obey and conform to the said orders, they will enjoy the same privileges as the natural born subjects of the King and they can count on our protection." Amherst requested that, when possible, militia captains should peacefully resolve any conflicts arising among the new subjects since nothing had been settled regarding the civil laws in force. Until a peace treaty had been signed, the land could not be considered to have been definitively ceded to England, which explains why the new leaders made few important decisions.

Trade was supposedly free but permits were required and the local governor had to approve any travel from one government to another. The colony had three governments, Montreal, Trois-Rivières, and Quebec, and foreign trade was obviously now under the exclusive control of the English. The most acute economic problem facing the Canadians was currency. For decades the scarcity of coins, owing mainly to unpredictable shipping conditions, had forced people to use card money or ordinance letters as tender. Many merchants and inhabitants had no other currency, but the English refused such tender or, at best, awarded only a small fraction of its original value, arguing that on October 15, 1759, the King of France had decreed that the paper currency was of no value.

The occupying military authorities forced the Canadian inhabitants to accommodate the English troops in their homes. Some women fell under the charms of the foreign soldiers as happens in all military occupations. The priest of Sainte-Anne-de-la-Pérade denounced the "scandal of a few debauched women who cavorted with English soldiers." Women who lived as concubines with soldiers were denied the sacraments because the clergy feared the consequences of mixed marriages on practice of the Catholic faith.

Roman Catholicism was not openly tolerated in England at that time. Lord Egremont, who was responsible for colonies, believed that "papism" was a serious error. On December 12, 1761, Egremont demanded that Amherst warn local governors "to give the strictest orders to prevent Soldiers, Mariners, and others among His Majesty's Subjects, from insulting or reviling any of the French Inhabitants, now their fellow Subjects, either by ungenerous insinuation of that Inferiority, which the fate of War has decided, or by harsh and provoking observations on their language, dress, Manners, Customs, or Country, or by uncharitable Reflections on the Errors of that mistaken Religion, which they unhappily profess." A position of this nature did not bode well for the Catholic clergy, particularly regarding the appointment of a new bishop to replace Monsignor Henri-Marie Dubrel de Pontbriand deceased in June 1760. Six years would go by before, in virtual secrecy, Jean-Olivier Briand was appointed the seventh bishop of the Quebec Diocese. However Bishop Briand's ability to exercise even the slightest authority depended entirely on the good will of Governor James Murray.

The fate of the former French colony was determined only after peace was reached on February 10, 1763. That treaty, known as the Treaty of Paris, was drafted and signed in French only. Article 4 stipulates: "his Most Christian Majesty cedes and guaranties to his said Britannick Majesty, in full right, Canada, with all its dependencies, as well as the island of Cape Breton, and all the other islands and coasts in the gulph and river of St. Lawrence, and in general, every thing that depends on the said countries." It clearly states that the cession is definitive and adds "His Britannick Majesty, on his side, agrees to grant the liberty of the Catholick religion to the inhabitants of Canada: he will, in consequence, give the most precise and most effectual orders, that his new Roman Catholic subjects may profess the worship of their religion according to the rites of the Romish church, as far as the laws of Great Britain permit." The rub, however, was that those laws of Great Britain allowed nothing! This problem had to be attended to.

Article 4 of the treaty also granted people, for an 18-month period, the right to return to France or, if they were Canadian born, to settle in the colony. The colony thus lost its elite comprised of seigneurs, merchants, and the wealthy in general. The Royal Proclamation of October 7 clarified some outstanding issues. "The Province of Quebec," as it became termed by the English, with its narrow borders, would be entitled to a Legislative Assembly when the authorities deemed it appropriate. Furthermore, permission to establish courts was granted "for hearing and determining all Causes, as well Criminal as Civil, according to Law and Equity, and as near as may be agreeable to the Laws of England." This necessarily raised the issue of the French civil laws that had applied for generations and under which contracts and other documents had been drafted for sales, purchases, wills, marriages, and much more.

With a tiny English population, it was out of the question to assimilate the Canadians. Nonetheless, in 1766 the Attorney General of the province, Francis Maseres, held that the only way to eliminate the growing conflict between French and English speakers was simply to assimilate those who spoke French. "Two nations are to be kept in peace and harmony, and moulded, as it were, into one that are at present of opposite religions, ignorant of each others language, and inclined in their affections to different systems of laws. The bulk of the inhabitants are hitherto either French from old France, or native Canadians, that speak only the French language, being, as it is thought, about ninety thousand souls, or as the French represent it in their Memorial, ten thousand heads of families. The rest of the inhabitants are natives of Great Britain or Ireland, or of the British dominions of North-America, and are at present only about six hundred souls; but, if the province is governed in such a manner as to give satisfaction by the accession of new settlers for the sake of trade and planting, so that in time they may equal or exceed the number of the French."

Some English speakers constantly petitioned for English laws to apply exclusively in the colony and for the right to do jury duty to be reserved for them only. They also demanded establishment of a Legislative Assembly to which elected membership was reserved exclusively to "old subjects." Catholics were already being excluded from positions in the public administration because they could not take the Test Oath under which they would have to forsake their faith.

Fortunately for the Canadians, however, rumblings in the Thirteen English Colonies to the south would hasten the resolution of these problems. The Crown was apprehensive about how the Canadians would react to any uprising by its subjects in New England. Some British jurists had also been studying the impact of continuing to apply French civil law.

The winds of revolution started blowing across the Thirteen Colonies in December 1773. The "populace of Boston," which was the expression used by the province of Quebec's first newspaper the *Gazette de Quebec*, had dumped cargoes of tea into the Boston harbour to protest a new tax. After the Boston Tea Party, Parliament in London passed five acts that the Americans described as the Intolerable Acts, the fifth being the Quebec Act. King George III gave Royal Sanction to it on June 22, 1774.

Under the Quebec Act, Quebec's territory was vastly expanded to include the Great Lakes hinterland, in the hope of keeping that land out of reach of the Thirteen Colonies. The governor was to be assisted by a legislative council comprising 17 to 23 members. French civil law was recognized but only English criminal law was to apply. The Canadians welcomed the Quebec Act as it confirmed the use of the civil law they knew and it put them under English criminal law and procedure. From that point on a person charged with a crime was innocent until the Crown proved him or her guilty, whereas previously under French law it was up to the person charged to prove his or her innocence. They also made gains concerning their religion. The Test Oath was abolished in the public administration, priests were entitled to tithe the population, and the freedom to profess the Catholic faith was granted "under the supremacy of the King."

The Quebec Act drew an enthusiastic reaction among the Canadians but it rubbed some of the King's "natural born subjects" the wrong way. The act came into force on April 30, 1775 despite the fact that the day before protesters in Montreal had blackened the bust of George III at Place d'Armes and put a necklace of potatoes on him with a cross bearing the inscription "Here is the pope of Canada or the English fool." Many people in the Thirteen Colonies demanded repeal of the Quebec Act. The Continental Congress in Philadelphia on October 21, 1774 approved the following address to the people of Great Britain. "Nor can we suppress our astonishment that a British Parliament should ever consent to establish in that country a religion that has deluged your island in blood, and dispersed impiety, bigotry, persecution, murder, and rebellion through every part of the world." Five days later delegates to the Continental Congress adopted the text of a letter addressed to the Canadians inviting them to become the fourteenth State of the future United States. After emphasizing all the injustice the "new subjects" had undergone, the congressmen promised to respect their laws and their religion and added dramatically, "Seize the opportunity presented to you by Providence itself. You have been conquered into liberty, if you act as you ought. This work is not of man. You are a small people compared to those who, with open arms, invite you into a fellowship. A moment's reflection should convince you which will be most for your interest and happiness, to have all the rest of North America your unalterable friends, or your inveterate enemies."

The Canadians must have taken too long to respond to their call because in 1775 two revolutionary armies invaded Quebec. The first, under the command of Richard Montgomery, descended the Richelieu River and seized Montreal virtually without a fight. The second, under the orders of Benedict Arnold, headed to Quebec City via the Chaudière River. In the midst of a raging snowstorm the invaders, decimated by disease, most likely smallpox, were defeated right under the walls of the Capital on December 31, 1775. They nonetheless laid siege to the city until navigation opened in the spring. The first ships brought 4800 German mercenaries to reinforce British troops who were bristling at the idea of fighting fellow Englishmen in the revolutionary armies.

Few Canadians relished the idea of defending their newly imposed ruler and some even took up arms in support of the revolutionaries. Fighting broke out on March 25, 1776 at Saint-Pierre-du-Sud near Montmagny downstream from Quebec on the south shore of the St. Lawrence. Loyal subjects of His Majesty King of England clashed with rebellious Canadians, thereby pitting fathers and sons and relatives against one another. Supporters of the American revolutionaries defied Bishop Briand's exhortations, fully aware that they ran the risk being denied the sacraments by taking up arms. Bishop Briand wrote to the priest of the Saint-Thomas de Montmagny parish ordering that "As regards sacraments, you shall give none, even at death, without renunciation and public reparations for the scandal, either to men or women; and those who die in their stubbornness, you shall not bury them in holy grounds without our permission, and should you bury them, which you are absolutely forbidden to do, you shall only attend in cassock, in surveillance not reciting any prayers, and the bodies shall not be allowed to enter the church, which we order you to keep closed except for during services." Bishop Briand's attitude was understandable under the religious teachings of the times. According to St. Paul, all authority stems from God, meaning that revolting against a duly established authority was the equivalent of revolting against God. British authority had been recognized by the Treaty of Paris of 1763 and was thus legally established, which meant that it was forbidden to take up arms against His Majesty. These teachings also partly explain the conduct of Bishop Jean-Jacques Lartigue of the Montreal Diocese during the Patriote uprising of 1837 and 1838. In both cases the Church sided with the British military authorities who in turn sided with the Church. The irony is that though many of the King's "natural born subjects" now living in Canada were virulently opposed to Catholicism, the British authorities had a good understanding with Church authorities and made common cause with them. This helps explain the strength and influence of the Catholic Church in Quebec right through until the 1960s.

Once the revolutionary troops had lifted siege and retreated, the British began to settle scores with the rebellious elements in the population. The Governor appointed three commissioners to judge the behaviour of the inhabitants and above all the militia captains' behaviour. Those captains who had been too soft or who had openly backed the invaders were removed from their positions. On Île d'Orleans, for example, some women had made impassioned speeches in support of the American revolutionaries and they were pejoratively nicknamed the "queens of Hungary."

The idea of invading Quebec resurfaced in 1778, a year after the French Marquis de La Fayette had thrown his support behind the Americans who, although they had declared their independence, still had to win it. The French Admiral Count Henri d'Estaing made another call for the Canadians to join forces with the American revolutionaries. "You were born French and you have not ceased to be French. [...] I shall not hold forth to an entire people, because an entire people, when it acquires the right to think and act, understands its interest; that joining the United States is to ensure its happiness; but I shall declare, as I declare solemnly in the name of His Majesty [Louis XVI] who authorized me to do so and ordered me to do so, that all his old subjects in North America who do not recognize the supremacy of England can count on his protection and his support." This inevitably heartened some Canadians who dreamed of France's return.

Governor Frederick Haldimand, who had been appointed in 1777, was a hard-nosed military officer who would stand for nothing that even resembled a rebellion or a conspiracy. He declared war on anybody who showed the slightest sympathy for the Americans or the French. Some went to jail including the Montreal merchant Pierre Du Calvet. After several years of detention, he went to London to obtain justice and later strongly supported British democratic institutions.

The United States and Great Britain signed a peace treaty on September 3, 1783, but thousands of people in the newly formed country wished to remain British subjects. They became known as Loyalists and emigrated mainly to Nova Scotia, which led to the creation of a new colony called New Brunswick. When 7000 Loyalists arrived in the province of Quebec, English colonial authorities welcomed them as martyrs, treated them with generosity, and granted them new lands in areas not under the seigneurial regime. The idea of honouring Canadian seigneurs was anathema to such loyal subjects of the King of England. The Loyalists also denounced the use of French civil law and the pervasive presence of the Catholic faith. Since they had been politically active in the Thirteen Colonies and were used to electing representatives to Parliament, they demanded the creation of an elected legislative assembly. This demand was also echoed by a large number of "new subjects," the Canadians, who were also intent on reforms and had petitioned for an elected assembly. Many of the changes demanded by the Loyalists however rankled the Canadians.

Until this point, the name "Canadians" only referred to the French-speaking subjects. In 1787, however, the postmaster Hugh Finlay claimed the right to be called a Canadian too. "Some people affect to call the King's Natural born subjects, *new Canadians*—He who chose, say they, to make Canada his place of residence lost the name of Englishman. The Old Canadians are those we conquer'd in 1760 and their descendants, the new Canadians are composed of emigrants from England, Scotland, Ireland, and the Colonies now the United States: by the Act of the 14th of his present Majesty (*The Quebec Act*) they are converted into Canadians, and Canadians they must remain." Several decades would go by however before English-speaking people would be called Canadians. Only then would the original French-speaking Canadians start to be known as "French Canadians."

Since the Loyalists had fled or were chased from a new country where republican ideas prevailed, and also found themselves in a neighbouring country where the land regime was totally different and the French language remained strong, they demanded a separate district in which they would feel at home. The Loyalists' demands compounded by the model established by the United States, prompted authorities in London to introduce parliamentary institutions in the Province of Quebec. The House of Commons in London thus studied a bill to this effect. Since the Loyalists demanded a "separate district" from that of the Canadians, it was decided to divide the province of Quebec into two territories, with the eastern part having a French-speaking majority and the western part, an English-speaking Loyalist majority. The border would be drawn along the western limits of the last seigneury which was Vaudreuil, located to the west of the island of Montreal. The name "Province of Quebec" thus disappeared and was replaced by two new names, Lower Canada and Upper Canada, in reference to their location on the St. Lawrence River.

Both Lower and Upper Canada were to have their own Parliament, an important new development. For Prime Minister William Pitt the Younger the new Constitution would result in the assimilation of the Canadians. He declared that the "French subjects" would be convinced that the British Government had no intention of imposing English laws on them. They would then reconsider with a free spirit their own laws and customs. He added that with time they would adopt English laws because they had become convinced about them. It was much better to proceed that way, according to Pitt the Younger, than to subject all the inhabitants of Canada to the Constitution and the laws of England. Experience would show them, he maintained, that English laws were "superior." Whatever the case, they had to be governed in a manner that satisfied them.

The Constitutional Act received Royal Sanction on June 10, 1791, effectively establishing a Legislative Council and a Legislative Assembly in both Upper and Lower Canada. Lower Canada's Assembly would have 50 members. The act set forth the conditions for a person to be eligible to hold a position as a representative of the people. Members would be elected based on a majority of votes cast by voters who had to be at least 21 years old and be British subjects by birth, conquest or naturalization. In addition, they could not have been convicted of treason or a felony. Since the Act uses the word "person," women who met the same criteria as men had the right to vote. This right would officially disappear in 1849, even though women had stopped voting several years before that date.

When the first elections were held in summer 1792, Lower Canada had 20 ridings. People went to the polls on different days, which thus enabled unsuccessful candidates to run in other ridings. Since voters would declare the name of the person for whom they wished to vote in a loud and clear voice to the returning officer who would record the vote in a special register, everybody knew who was in the lead. Each riding had a single polling station that remained open until one hour had gone by without any voters showing up. An election could last several days. People soon realized that supporters of one candidate only had to block the road to the polling station to ensure victory.

With a majority in Lower Canada speaking French, the issue of English representation came to the fore. A correspondent with the *Quebec Herald* expressed his fears to his fellow English who had demanded a Legislative Assembly. He asked whether, in their demands for an assembly, they had thought about the fact that the Canadians outnumbered the Englishman 20 to 1 in the Province of Quebec. He insisted that in current conditions a person could bet 50 to 1 that the Canadians would not elect a single Englishman and that it was very careless to petition so that other masters could govern them. The author of the article, a certain John Bull, was mistaken. When voting was over the English, who represented only 10 percent of the population, found themselves with a third of the Assembly members. Several reasons explain these results. Some Canadians were convinced that the English would represent them better because of their long experience with the parliamentary system. Moreover with voting taking place in the open and candidates being chosen from among employers, seigneury owners, or lenders, it would be dangerous for Canadians to refuse to vote for such influential people.

The first session of the first Parliament began on December 17, 1792 and immediately the question of ethnic origin and language was raised. The Speaker was to be of what nationality? Would a Canadian qualify for the position or would it be held by an "old subject?" Member Joseph Papineau observed "that it could not be assumed that any Canadian should be denied his rights because he did not understand English." Jean-Antoine Panet was elected Speaker with 28 votes in favour and 18 against. Three French-speaking members voted with the English-speaking members.

Members and voters did not immediately realize that the Parliamentary system would soon be a double-edged sword. Historian Lionel Groulx qualified the new system as being gerrymandered, claiming that Parliament and Democracy were by no means synonymous. All bills adopted by the Legislative Assembly had to be approved by the Legislative Council whose members were appointed for life by authorities in England. The final decision fell to the Governor who could grant Royal Sanction to the bill, reject it, or suspend its adoption for up to two years awaiting the King's decision. This process meant that members lacked any real power. A day would come when they would unequivocally demand more power, especially when they realized that they controlled neither the legislative process nor the budget.

The Province of Quebec was divided into two separate colonies named Upper and Lower Canada and both were granted legislative assemblies in 1791. The first debate in Lower Canada's Legislative Assembly illustrated here was on the status of the French language which until then had no official status.

The Port of Montreal bustled with activity in the middle of the 19th century.

CHAPTER 6

Heading for Confrontation

France and Great Britain went to war again in early
February 1793 at a time when revolution in France was producing more and more casualties. English authorities in
Lower Canada feared the arrival of French spies, especially
because revolutionaries in Paris were petitioning for the
recovery of lands that the monarchy had abandoned. Citizen
Edmond-Charles Genêt, delegated by the government of
France to the Philadelphia Congress, wrote to Canadians on
behalf of the "Free French" with a clear invitation to rise up.
"Today we are free, we have reclaimed our rights, our oppres-
sors have been punished, all parts of our administration have
regenerated, and, strengthened by the justice of our cause, by
our courage and by the immense means with which we are
preparing to defeat all tyrants in the world, it is finally within
our power to avenge you and to render you as free as we are,
as independent as your neighbours the Americans of the
United States. Canadians, follow their example and ours, the
route has been cleared, and magnanimous determination can
make you leave the state of abjection in which you have been
plunged." Putting those words to action, a small French fleet
weighed anchor in Chesapeake Bay and set out to "liberate"
Quebec. It was already late in the year and stories of the harsh
Canadian winter prompted the commander to change course
and set sail for Bordeaux.

The French threat gave rise to a hunt for spies, foreigners, and French sympathizers. A new law was passed to reorganize the militia, a reform that upset many Canadians and resulted in loud demonstrations of disapproval. Another law on road maintenance provoked a similar reaction.

During the first years of the 19th century, tensions escalated between the two groups. The English authorities decided to intervene directly in education at the behest of Jacob Mountain, the Anglican Bishop of Quebec City. In 1799 Bishop Mountain complained that "This total ignorance of the English language, on the part of the Canadians, draws a distinct line of demarcation between them and His Majesty's British subjects in this Province, injurious to the welfare and happiness of both; and continues to divide into two separate people, those who by their situation, their common interests, and their equal participation of the same laws, and the same form of government, should naturally form but one." The schools of the "Royal Institution," adopted in 1801, were not very successful.

The Anglican Bishop was not alone in proposing that Lower Canada become English. The columns of the weekly *Quebec Mercury* regularly ran attacks on the Canadians. In the edition published on October 27, 1806, a certain "Anglicanus" bluntly stated that "This province is already too much a French province for an English colony. To *unfrenchify* it, as much as possible, if I may be allowed the phrase, should be a primary object, [...] My complaint, is against the unavoidable result of an unnecessary cultivation of the french language, in a country, where common policy requires its diminution, rather than its further dissemination. [...] After forty seven years possession of Quebec it is time the Province should be english." To answer these attacks, the Canadian leaders launched the first newspaper published in French only, *Le Canadien,* whose goal was to avenge the honour of the Canadians. The promotional flyer stated ironically: "We have committed crimes against them, we have even made them use their mother tongue to express their feelings and to obtain justice, but accusations only frighten the guilty; true expression of loyalty is loyal in all tongues, while expression of disloyalty, of lowliness, and of envy, expression that sows division among fellow citizens called upon to live as brothers, also dishonours all languages."

The fight raging between the *Quebec Mercury* and *Le Canadien* echoed what was happening in the Legislative Assembly. Although there were no political parties yet, the demarcation between representatives of the two groups was becoming more and more distinct. French-speaking members denounced the fact that the judges who were appointed by the government could also be elected and sit as members of Parliament. It represented a dangerous marriage between the legislative and judicial branches. The election of Ezekial Hart, a Jew, was also contested, although opposition stemmed not mainly from his religion but from the fact that he was close to the English.

Governor James Craig was a military officer appointed in 1807 who held the demands of French-speaking members in deep contempt. Craig also tended to see conspiracies everywhere, but he nonetheless managed to keep abreast of changing mentalities. Some people in his entourage proposed to adopt measures to assimilate the French-speaking population as quickly as possible, such as uniting Upper and Lower Canada with weighted representation favouring the British minority so that they would hold a majority in the Legislative Assembly.

Craig ordered the arrest of the publishers of *Le Canadien* on the grounds that it was a seditious publication. In a letter to British authorities dated May 1, 1810, he pointed out how the Canadians saw themselves: "their habits, their language and their religion, have remained as distinct from ours as they were before the conquest. Indeed, it seems to be a favourite object with them to be considered as a separate Nation; *La Nation Canadienne* is their constant expression, and with regard to their having been hitherto quiet and faithful subjects, it need only be observed that no opportunity has been presented them and encouragement to shew themselves otherwise."

The opportunity came in 1812 when war broke out between the United States and Great Britain. France and Great Britain had been at war for some time but the United States had remained neutral. It was feared that their entry in the war might lead to an invasion of the two Canadas. The Canadians' loyalty to the new mother country would prove to be almost unconditional. The Canadian Voltigeurs headed by Charles-Michel Iroumberry de Salaberry took an active part in the victorious battle of Châteauguay on October 26, 1813.

In Western Europe the tides of war ebbed and flowed with the Emperor Napoleon winning some battles and losing others. In an attempt to prevent Britain from developing her navy, Napoleon decreed a blockade on all trade with Great Britain in November 1806 thus forcing Great Britain to procure its timber supplies elsewhere than in the Nordic countries. Upper and Lower Canada became the main suppliers, and this marked the economic turning point when the forest industry largely took over from the fur trade as the pillar of the colonies. The Canadians went from being mainly trappers and fur traders to being lumberjacks. The Ottawa River Valley was the first region logged. Timber was assembled to form rafts or cages and was driven down the Ottawa River and the St. Lawrence to Quebec City where it was loaded on ships headed for Great Britain. The raftsmen, known also as "cageux" in French, became the stuff of legend. The most famous of all was Joseph "Jos" Montferrand, a Montrealer who made a name for himself working the Ottawa River Valley and who became an early incarnation of Maurice Richard. Historian Fernand Ouellet considered this change in the economy of Lower Canada to be a turning point in French Canadian society. "The timber trade gave rise to a class of longshoremen. [...] It not only attracted capital and considerable investment, it also became the main source of earnings likely to be reinvested in the development of the colony. It represented the development of the first essentially English Canadian companies."

The Treaty of Ghent signed on December 24, 1814 in what is now Belgium put an end to the war between the United States and Great Britain. A month earlier some Canadians had sent a brief to the British authorities setting forth their demands: "As the mass of the people are Canadians, the majority in the Legislative Assembly consists of Canadians, whereas the English, with a few devoted Canadians, form the minority; and because the Canadians in the majority, freely elected by the people, were unable to show the devotion necessary, they were not allowed to take their seats. The members who were made executive councillors were chosen from among the minority." The majority felt slighted, and their demands became steadily more specific and were presented ever more energetically.

In the Legislative Assembly the majority of French-speaking members joined the Parti Canadien. This was the period when the first Canadian political parties were founded. Members of the Legislative Assembly looked up to Louis-Joseph Papineau who was elected Speaker in 1815 and soon became leader of the Parti Canadien. It had become clear that the only way for them to ensure that their demands reached the authorities in London was to go through the Governor. They had observed that their demands were being filtered and that those sent to London were accompanied by a "governmental" interpretation. A committee of the Assembly thus requested the appointment of an agent stressing that it was particularly necessary for the province of Lower Canada to appoint a person who would live in Great Britain. The goal was to counter the uneasiness among the inhabitants of Lower Canada at a time when they feared efforts were being deployed that would prompt the imperial government and the English nation to be prejudicial towards them. The committee thought it possible that a constitutional change contrary to the "English wisdom" contained in the existing Constitution might be imposed through union of the provinces of Upper and Lower Canada, whose languages, laws, and customs were totally different. According to the committee the uneasiness would disappear if a resident agent were appointed in England. The committee's demand remained unanswered, for the time being.

The fear that Westminster might be misinformed by English-speaking people in Upper and Lower Canada would be echoed shortly thereafter by Alexis de Tocqueville in a letter to a friend who was clerk of the Privy Council in London. Replying to a request for advice on how the Crown should respond to the 1837 rebellion, de Tocqueville wrote: "In short, my dear friend, do not trust what the English who have settled in Canada nor the Americans from the United States have to say about the Canadien population. Their views are coloured by incredible prejudice and any government that would take those views only would be courting disaster."

The question of judges sitting as members of the Assembly had yet to be settled. Another issue arose in 1818, namely the control of public expenditures, which came to be known as the "quarrel over subsidies." In Great Britain, the civil list, or the salaries granted to civil servants, was adopted as a block and applied throughout the Sovereign's life. The Lower Canada Assembly members wanted to study each case and vote for the civil list detail by detail because they knew that some people were receiving amounts for tasks that they had not accomplished. They also wanted to put an end to sinecures. In short, they were fighting to participate in the control of government spending, including the civil list, since subsidies were requested to pay for the list. The quarrel over subsidies regularly paralysed the Assembly but produced no results. The governors' attitudes varied depending on the personality of the man in office.

The sharing of customs revenue between Upper and Lower Canada gave rise to another problem. Since all merchandise arrived at the Quebec City port, even cargoes destined for Upper Canada, some people believed that uniting the two colonies would solve the problem. Parliament in London studied a bill in 1822 proposing their union and the creation of a single Legislative Assembly and a single Legislative Council. In Lower Canada the possibility of increasing the number of electoral ridings by creating new ridings in the townships was discussed. With the arrival of Loyalists and new immigrants from Great Britain, new lands had to be cleared for settlement and agriculture. These lands were located beyond the areas covered by the seigneurial regime. Townships were thus created, usually covering square plots measuring 10 miles by 10 miles. The land was granted in free and common socage, which meant that those receiving lots paid neither rent nor seigneurial dues of any kind. They became the land owners. Many of these townships were located south and south-east of Montreal and were known as the Eastern Townships. The word "Eastern" referred to the fact that they were to the east of the townships granted in Upper Canada.

The idea that Upper and Lower Canada might be united sparked controversy. Unionists vaunted the advantages of the project while opponents of union, primarily Canadians, spoke of its dangers. While dozens of petitions were sent to London, Louis-Joseph Papineau and John Neilson crossed the Atlantic to explain in person why the two colonies should not be united. When they arrived in London, the bill had been tabled. The two delegates observed however that the unionist representative Andrew Stuart was applying tremendous pressure to have the bill passed. Stuart had submitted a fiery brief in which he claimed that Lower Canada was mainly inhabited by a population that could be considered foreign, even though more than 60 years had gone by since the Conquest. In his opinion this population had made no progress towards assimilation with their fellow citizens of British extraction. Some English-speaking residents of Lower Canada were dissatisfied with developments and demanded that Lower Canada be partitioned so that the island of Montreal would be attached to Upper Canada. Certain groups believed that the solution was to unite all the English colonies in North America.

The attitude of the majority of French-speaking members towards the subsidies virtually paralysed work in the Legislative Assembly in Quebec City. Louis-Joseph Papineau was assuming an increasingly dominant position. Papineau was the leader of the Parti Canadien, which became the Parti Patriote in 1926, although some people occasionally attempted to challenge him, particularly in the Quebec City area where he had a reputation for being too radical.

Two very different events occurred in 1832 to aggravate matters in Lower Canada. A by-election in Montreal, conducted under the regular electoral rules, had lasted more than 20 days. It pitted Daniel Tracey, the pro-Patriote Irish doctor who ran the newspaper *The Vindicator*, against Stanley Bagg, who was supported by Loyalists. People feared the worst especially when the army was deployed to maintain law and order. When a disturbance broke out on Monday May 21, the army shot at the crowd and killed three demonstrators, all French-speaking Montrealers. The French-language newspaper, *La Minerve*, published a blistering denunciation. "Never forget the massacre of our brothers; all Canadians must transmit from father to son for generations to come the scenes that took place on the 21st of this month; the names of the perverse people who planned, advised, and executed this killing must be fully chronicled, alongside the names of our defenders in such a manner that the former go down in disgrace and shame and that the latter be remembered by our great grandchildren with honour and distinction." The Governor, Lord Aylmer, fanned the flames of revolt by quite astonishingly congratulating the officers who gave orders to fire on the crowd.

Daniel Tracey won the by-election but never sat in the Legislative Assembly since he died on July 18 in an epidemic that ravaged Lower Canada. Cholera had struck in June 1832 killing more than 10,000 people including Tracey. The epidemic was believed to have originated with the massive arrival of mostly Irish immigrants. Members of the Parti Canadien suspected that political leaders in Great Britain were trying to decimate the Canadian population. The people of Lower Canada, the clergy, and the religious orders nonetheless provided remarkable aid and relief to the immigrants that teemed out of the ships. A population census in 1831 showed that Lower Canada had a population of 583,000, with 43,700 living in Montreal and 27,100 in Quebec City. The majority of the people in Lower Canada were farmers residing in rural areas.

French and English language newspapers regularly ran stories about independence movements in Latin America and about the many revolutions that were changing the face of Western Europe. Leaders in Lower and Upper Canada followed those events closely and "sovereignty of the people" became a sharply debated issue. The Bishop of Montreal, Jean-Jacques Lartigue, considered this "right" to be a fundamental error. On the other hand, a young lawyer by the name of Pierre Winters strongly defended the idea in a letter to newspaper publisher Ludger Duvernay of *La Minerve* on September 30, 1833. "I hope that we shall stop humbly petitioning and that we shall speak like free men or at least like men born to be free. Thus I hope that the universal cry from one end of the country to the other will be 'freedom or death' and that we shall sing 'Live Free or Die'."

Tensions escalated the following year when the Parti Patriote led by Louis-Joseph Papineau published its list of demands. Among their "Ninety-two Resolutions," the members of the Legislative Assembly demanded an elected legislative council, expulsion of judges from the Executive Council, control of the civil list, and much more. Their denunciations also targeted the stacking or plurality of responsibilities, army intervention during elections, increased government spending, and poor management of Crown lands. Adding to the agitation, another cholera epidemic struck and in its wake left some 600 people dead. The general elections held in fall 1834 bore witness to the widespread discontent among the French-speaking people of Canada. The Parti Patriote won 77 of the 88 seats in the Legislative Assembly.

Events in Lower Canada began to irritate imperial authorities in London. Archibald Acheson, Count of Gosford, was appointed Governor of Upper and Lower Canada with the mission of investigating and reporting on the situation in the two colonies. Troubles were not confined to Lower Canada as agitation was also spreading to Upper Canada. In an attempt to curry favour among Canadians who backed Papineau, the King's new representative invited a majority of French-speaking people to celebrate St. Catherine's Day on November 25, 1835. Reactionary English Montrealers saw this as pandering and loudly expressed their disapproval.

Adam Thom, a journalist with the Montreal Herald, rang the alarm and called on English people to prepare for an uprising by the Canadians. "The French faction's rashness and your lordship's weakness have rendered the struggle no longer political but purely national," wrote Thom using the nom de plume of Camillus in reference to the Roman General who defeated the Gauls after they had taken Rome. "A French state shall not be permitted to exist on this English continent. Five hundred thousand determined men will speedily repeat that declaration in voices of thunder."

Within weeks, when 200 or more banner-carrying English citizens marching to music converged at a meeting, it was clearly a call to arms. An armed group marched through the streets of Montreal shortly thereafter marking the founding of the Doric Club. A toast was proposed: "Death rather than French domination." In reply, the Patriote newspaper La Minerve called for vigilance on December 10, 1835. "We believe it best for us to organize to avoid being caught off guard and also to be prepared to face them should they attempt to riot."

Until this point Papineau's supporters, the Patriotes, believed that Governor Gosford was somewhat sympathetic to their demands. They learned however that for Parliament in London an elected Legislative Council was out of the question and that marked the end of the "bonne entente" or good understanding. They were now headed straight for confrontation and the crisis reached a climax when London adopted a series of resolutions in April 1837. On the initiative of Lord John Russell, Secretary of State for the Colonies, Parliament had adopted extreme measures to end the quarrel over subsidies and, Russell thought, settle the problems in Lower Canada once and for all. An elected Legislative Council was ruled out, as was responsible government under which the ministers in the Council would be held accountable for their decisions before the Legislative Assembly. Russell's eighth resolution, however, was the spark that ignited the fire. It authorized the Governor to take funds from the Legislative Assembly when necessary and without its authorization to pay for "the established and customary charges of the administration of justice, and of the civil government of the said province."

When these resolutions became known in Lower Canada, Papineau and his supporters immediately began to mobilize. Since import duties were among the main sources of revenue for the colony, they called on people to boycott all imported goods. The journalist and assembly member Edmund Bailey O'Callaghan pointed out that the goods shipped to Quebec City would be illegally distributed by the British parliament and represented royalties that were taken for the brandy, rum, wine, tobacco, tea and other such articles. He invited his fellow country men who needed a stimulant to drink locally distilled whisky and to encourage the smuggling of tea, tobacco, and other articles from the United States. For O'Callaghan that was the only solution because it would deprive England of revenue obtained illegally and unconstitutionally and thereby paralyse the oppressor's actions in Canada. "Contraband!" became their rallying cry.

In the following months meetings were held to protest Russell's resolutions and Louis-Joseph Papineau rose as the most convincing speaker and the person most sought after. An emergency meeting of the Executive Council was called to adopt a proclamation prohibiting these seditious assemblies, but the proclamation was ignored. The June 24 Saint-Jean-Baptiste festivities, which had been declared official in 1834, began to resemble an anti-British celebration. Members of the Legislative Assembly were convened for a new session in mid-August. Many entered the Legislative Assembly dressed in cloth of the country to demonstrate their refusal to wear imported material. Governor Gosford suspended the Constitution in force on the grounds that he had no other choice and applied a quasi military rule in the colony.

The Doric Club multiplied its activities and its members regularly paraded fully armed through the streets of Montreal. Young Patriotes refused to ignore these provocations and decided to found a rival organization, the *Fils de la Liberté* or Sons of Freedom. A new English-speaking group, the British Rifle Corps, was then launched with the avowed goal of providing military support to the regular troops in case of an uprising and it claimed to be capable of arming and mobilizing 1200 men.

Patriotic assemblies or rallies were held everywhere and, following debates and voting, produced resolutions directly challenging the government. The largest rally attended by thousands of people took place at Saint-Charles, in the Richelieu River Valley east of Montreal. A freedom tree was planted adorned with a Phrygien or Liberty Cap, made famous during the American and French revolutions. Armed militiamen stood at attention when Papineau dressed in cloth of the country took the stage. In a powerful speech, he proposed to the crowd to pursue the constitutional means that had not yet been exhausted, which was a subtle warning against taking up arms as some were already suggesting. Wolfred Nelson, who led the Patriotes of neighbouring Saint-Denis, believed otherwise. "Well I differ with Mr. Papineau," he declared. "I maintain that the time has arrived to cast our tin spoons and plates into bullets." The 5000 people attending the rally realized that the banner of revolt had been rolled out. The very next day Bishop Lartigue reacted by publishing a peremptory order for the population to accept British authority. "Do not allow yourselves to be seduced if someone might try to engage you in rebellion against the established government, under the pretence that you are part of the Sovereign People." He brandished the threat of denying a Christian burial to those who might die with weapons in their hands.

Acting quickly, Governor Gosford issued arrest warrants for 26 Patriotes on November 16, 1837, and offered a reward for the arrest of Louis-Joseph Papineau. Since the Patriotes in Saint-Charles had started to build fortifications, orders were given to the army to march on that town before it was too late. The army arrived at Saint-Denis, the town just downstream on the Richelieu River from Saint-Charles, on November 23. Wolfred Nelson and his group of poorly armed Patriotes managed to beat back the advancing army. Papineau had left the town shortly before the confrontation and would later be accused of having fled the battle. The Patriotes were defeated two days later on November 25, after which the British troops and English-speaking irregulars wreaked havoc and destruction throughout the area. A few weeks later on December 14 the Patriotes of Saint-Eustache, in the Deux-Montagnes area northwest of Montreal, were also defeated and brutalized by British soldiers when they sought refuge in the Church. It is worth noting that the Patriotes did not initiate fighting in 1837. They only attempted to resist and stop the advancing

British troops. Some historians have argued that the Patriotes were provoked into taking up arms so that the British could put them down once and for all.

The following year was a completely different story. Papineau was in retreat and divisions plagued the Patriotes who had escaped arrest by seeking refuge in the United States. Robert Nelson took over as leader of the Patriotes who wanted to continue fighting. During a brief incursion into Lower Canada on February 28, 1838, Nelson proclaimed the independence of the Republic of Lower Canada. The text proclaimed that all citizens, including the "Savages," would have equal rights, the Church and the state would be separated, and the seigneurial regime, abolished. The death penalty would only apply in cases of murder, the press would be free, elections would be held with secret ballots, and the French and English languages would be used in all public matters. The Patriote movement, it should be remembered, had many English-speaking members as well as Europeans inspired by the winds of Liberty that were blowing throughout the world. Furthermore, under the leadership of William Lyon Mackenzie another uprising had shaken Upper Canada during the same period.

The revolt in the fall of 1838 failed and hundreds of Patriotes were thrown in jail. After summary military trials, 12 Patriotes were hanged in Lower Canada and more than 50 were banished to New South Wales in Australia. Their banishment gave rise to a famous lament *Un Canadien errant*, that was popularized in the 20th century by Paul Robeson and Leonard Cohen, among others. In Upper Canada 17 rebels were executed and another 130 were deported.

The fight for freedom led by Papineau and the Parti Patriote cut a broad swath nonetheless. One striking example was the Jewish Emancipation Act of June 5, 1832. This "act to declare persons professing the Jewish religion entitled to all the rights and privileges of the other subjects of his majesty in this province" was a first in the British Empire. In fact 27 years went by before the Parliament in London passed similar legislation granting Jews full political and social rights. The question had come to the fore when Ezekiel Hart was elected to the Legislative Assembly in 1807 in his home riding of Trois-Rivières. When Hart declined to take the Christian oath of office, he was refused the right to sit. The people of Trois-Rivières re-elected him a year later only to see him expelled once again, although the main reason for his expulsion was that he had voted with the Bureaucrats and was close to Governor James Craig. For some 20 years thereafter Jews continued to live in a legal vacuum since they were allowed no official register for births, deaths, and marriages. In 1828 a petition to the legislature requested that Jews be allowed to keep their own registers and to constitute themselves as a community. This led to the law establishing the Montreal Jewish Community and another petition regarding the right for Jews to hold public office. Louis-Joseph Papineau and the Patriotes ensured that the act was adopted virtually unopposed. For the first time, Jews became magistrates. Moreover, when the leaders of the Patriote rebellion were tried by a military tribunal in 1838, a nephew of Ezekiel Hart, Aaron Philip Hart came to the defence of a Patriote by the name of Joseph-Narcisse Cardinal. Despite martial law that prevented him from speaking up, Hart made a courageous four-hour plea that convinced the court to spare Cardinal's life, but interim Governor John Colborne quickly overturned the decision. Cardinal and Joseph Duquet were thus found guilty of high treason and hanged. The day before their execution on December 21, 1838, Aaron Hart and his colleague L.T. Drummond wrote the Governor warning that the trial was "illegal, unconstitutional, and unjust." In risking his life and future to defend the Patriotes Cardinal and Duquet, Hart was protesting the brutal repression of those who had enabled Jews to obtain equality.

After the clash in 1837 and before the 1838 revolt, London sent a new investigator by the name of Lord Durham to Canada to study the situation. After hastily returning to England Lord Durham published his famous report. Although Durham would have preferred uniting all the British colonies in North America, his two main recommendations called for the union of Upper and Lower Canada and the sending of as many immigrants as possible to the colony. If these two recommendations were applied, he submitted, the gradual assimilation of the French-speaking population would be facilitated because they would effectively be made into a minority with the union of the two colonies. His outlook on French Canadians became famous. "They form a people without history and without literature." He added: "The language, the laws and the character of the North American continent are English and every other race than the English race is in a state of inferiority. It is in order to release them from this inferiority that I wish to give the Canadians our English character."

On one point Lord Durham was not totally off the mark. Until that point the Canadians had no written history. François-Xavier Garneau would remedy that problem with his book *L'Histoire du Canada de sa découverte jusqu'à nos jours* (*The History of Canada from Discovery until the Present Day*) published in 1845.

London took Durham's recommendations very seriously when it adopted the Act of Union to which Queen Victoria granted Royal Sanction on July 23, 1840. Upper and Lower Canada now formed a single Province of Canada, also known as United Canada. The colony would have a single Legislative

Assembly comprising 84 members, with 42 coming from each of the former colonies. This represented a flagrant injustice for Lower Canada where the primarily French-speaking population outnumbered the primarily English-speaking population of Upper Canada by more than 200,000. It became obvious that a majority of members of the future Parliament would speak English, whereas the majority of the population in the new United Canada spoke French.

The debts of the two colonies were also consolidated into a single debt, which represented still another injustice since Upper Canada had incurred an enormous debt of some 1.2 million sterling pounds (louis) for the construction of roads and buildings. Lower Canada, on the other hand, owed only 95,000 sterling pounds because of the quarrel over subsidies that had virtually paralysed civil administration. In a nutshell, the people of Lower Canada were forced to pay for the development of the neighbouring colony. The final injustice was Article 41 that made English the only official language of government. Quebec historian Denis Vaugeois quite accurately describes the Act of Union as the "second conquest."

4,000 Piastres de Recompense !

GOSFORD.

Province du Bas-Canada.

Par son Excellence le Très-Honorable ARCHIBALD, COMTE DE GOSFORD, Baron Worlingham de Beccles, au Comté de Suffolk, Capitaine Géneral et Gouverneur en Chef dans et pour les Provinces du Bas-Canada et du Haut-Canada, Vice-Amiral d'icelles, et Conseiller de Sa Majesté en son Très-Honorable Conseil privé, &c. &c. &c.

PROCLAMATION.

ATTENDU que, par information sous serment, il appert que,

LOUIS JOSEPH PAPINEAU,

de la cité de Montréal, Ecuyer, est accusé du crime de Haute Trahison ; Et attendu que le dit Louis Joseph Papineau s'est retiré du lieu de sa résidence ordinaire, et qu'il y a raison de croire qu'il a fui la justice ; et attendu qu'il est expédient et nécessaire à la due administration de la justice et à la sécurité du Gouvernement de Sa Majesté, en cette Province, qu'un si grand crime ne reste pas impuni. A ces causes, sachez que je, le dit Archibald, Comte de Gosford, de l'avis du Conseil Exécutif de Sa Majesté pour cette Province, ai jugé à propos de faire sortir cette Proclamation, et par icelle je requiers tous sujets affectionnés de Sa Majesté en cette Province, et leur commande de découvrir, prendre et appréhender le dit Louis Joseph Papineau, en quelque lieu qu'il se trouve en icelle, et de l'amener devant un juge désigné pour conserver la paix, ou Magistrat Principal, dans l'une ou l'autre des cités de Québec ou de Montréal susdit ; Et pour encourager toutes personnes à être diligentes à s'efforcer de découvrir et d'appréhender le dit Louis Joseph Papineau, et à l'amener devant tel Juge désigné pour conserver la Paix ou Magistrat comme susdit, j'offre par les présentes une

RECOMPENSE DE

MILLE LIVRES,

du cours de cette Province, à quiconque appréhendera ainsi le dit Louis Joseph Papineau et le livrera entre les mains de la Justice.

Donné sous mon Seing et le Sceau des mes Armes, au Château St. Louis, dans la cité de Québec, le premier jour de Decembre dans l'année de Notre Seigneur mil huit cent trente sept, et dans la première année du règne de Sa Majesté.

Par Ordre de Son Excellence,

(Signé,) D. DALY,
Secrétaire de la Province.

Imprimée par JOHN CHARLTON FISHER, et WILLIAM KEMBLE, Imprimeur de sa Mté &c.

On December 1, 1837, a reward of 4000 piastres or 1000 pounds was offered for the arrest of the Patriote leader Louis-Joseph Papineau. Since June 1837, rewards had already been offered for different members of the Patriote Party.

On December 14, 1837, Colborne led some 6000 troops and irregulars to quell resistance by the Patriotes at Saint-Eustache to the northwest of Montreal. After the Patriotes took refuge in the church and surrounding buildings, Colborne attacked and killed many of the Patriotes, threw the women and children out of their homes, and set fire to them and to buildings throughout the area. The church in Saint-Eustache still shows the marks of Colborne's attack.

CHAPTER 7

A New Constitution
in the Offing

The original Canadians began to identify themselves, or be identified, as French Canadians since many English-speaking inhabitants were calling themselves Canadians. A new battle was brewing over the adverse effects of the new Constitution and it thrust Louis-Hyppolyte La Fontaine to the forefront. In a manifesto published in August 1840 as general elections approached, La Fontaine set forth his views on the Union. "Union has been decreed! Canada, in the thinking of the English Parliament, shall in the future consist of but one province. Is this important political measure in the interest of the populations to whom it proposes to be submitted to the action of a single and same legislature? Time alone will be able resolve this problem."

Union also meant that the two colonies would have a single capital in Kingston, thus achieving the objective of establishing it near Lower Canada but not in it. When the first sessions began some members demanded responsible government. La Fontaine championed the fight along with Robert Baldwin, Upper Canada's leading political figure. The two leaders formed a team and in 1842 Governor Charles Bagot invited them to join the Cabinet. When La Fontaine made his first speech in French on September 13, 1842, a member from

Toronto demanded that he speak English, to which La Fontaine retorted: "He has asked me to make my first speech in this Chamber in a tongue other than my mother tongue! I refuse with all my energy to make the speech in English. I must nonetheless inform the honourable member and the other honourable members and the general public of the sense of justice that I do not fear to invoke in saying that, even if I were as familiar with the English language as I am with the French language, I would still insist on making my first speech in the tongue of my French Canadian countrymen, if only to protest solemnly against the cruel injustice of the Act of Union that tends to prohibit the mother tongue of half of the population of Canada. I owe it to my fellow countrymen and I owe it to myself."

A majority of members voted against making Kingston the seat of government, but certain members from ridings in Upper Canada bristled at the idea of making Montreal the capital. One newspaper in Upper Canada complained that to have the seat of government transferred beyond the boundaries of Upper Canada would be even worse than annexation by the United States because it would be proof that the French were taking power. Violence broke out during the 1844 general elections and the army was called in to Montreal to restore order.

During the following session a majority of members adopted an act to indemnify inhabitants of Upper Canada who had suffered losses during the revolt of 1837. La Fontaine had demanded that a similar measure be voted for Lower Canada, but was unsuccessful... for the time being. By that time most of the Lower Canada Patriotes exiled in New South Wales had returned or were about to do so.

In Lower Canada thousands of new Irish immigrants openly showed their support for the French Canadians. Each year the Port of Quebec teemed with new arrivals. Scores of people headed straight for the United States or for Upper Canada but a large number settled in the St. Lawrence Valley. In Montreal, Irish Protestants and Catholics had their own parishes. For instance, the Parish of Saint-Patrick was created in Montreal for English-speaking Catholics. As the first ships arrived from Great Britain with people fleeing the famine that ravaged Ireland, disease also showed its face. A typhus epidemic left nearly 14,000 dead.

Political parties began to form and the question of a double majority was immediately raised. Was a government obliged, in order to remain in power, to hold a majority of seats in both parts of United Canada? Responsible government was also still a burning issue. At the same time some people advocated annexing Canada to the United States. Feeling that England had abandoned them by adopting free trade, they demanded that legislation forcing the colonies to conduct trade, imports, and exports exclusively with English ships be abolished. Such legislation ran counter to free trade, provoked anger among merchants, and exacerbated tensions between English and French.

In general elections in early 1848, Louis-Joseph Papineau, who had returned from exile in 1845, ran successfully for Parliament. A Montreal newspaper, *The Morning Courier*, wrote on January 26 that it was no longer a fight between Tories and Radicals, but rather a "war of races" and the question before them was whether the French Canadians would put their foot on the throats of Englishmen or if they would know why they exist, namely to hew wood and draw water. The confrontation occurred a year later. Responsible government became a fact. Article 41 of the Act of Union allowing English only in Parliament became obsolete. Moreover, Governor Elgin, who was Lord Durham's son-in-law, made the Throne speech in both languages.

With an economic crisis brewing the political situation deteriorated despite Governor Elgin's apparent good will. The bill to indemnify those in Lower Canada who had suffered losses during the revolts of 1837 and 1838 brought things to a boil. The main point of contention was the demand that indemnities be granted to those who had lost property due to the brutality of the troops and English-speaking irregulars. The beneficiaries were only those who had not been convicted by the courts in relation to the Patriote uprising. Proponents of the bill insisted that it was only natural to indemnify people in Lower Canada since the Legislative Assembly of Upper Canada had already indemnified those who had experienced similar losses following the rebellion in Upper Canada. Opponents to the bill however perceived it to be a reward for revolt. The Rebellion Losses Bill was adopted by the Legislative Assembly thanks to the solid majority held by the La Fontaine-Baldwin Government. It also garnered a majority of five votes in the Legislative Council. The question on everybody's lips was: will Governor Elgin grant the bill Royal Sanction? Hues and cries arose in Upper Canada against the idea of indemnifying the Patriotes. In one paper the call was clear: One of the two races, the Saxon or the French, had to disappear from Canada.

Despite apprehended agitation, Elgin granted Royal Sanction on Wednesday, April 25, 1849. *The Montreal Gazette* published a special flyer that afternoon that was an unfettered call to revolt: "The end has come. Anglo-Saxons, you must live for the future; your race and your blood shall be your supreme law, if you are true to yourselves." The flyer instructed the crowd to be English rather than British, and called on them to rally at Place d'Armes. Shortly after the rally, demonstrators sacked and set fire to the Parliament House located in the Marché Sainte-Anne at Place d'Youville in Old

Montreal. The leader of the mob was Alfred Perry who proudly described the feat in *The Montreal Star* years later. Ironically, Alfred Perry was a volunteer fireman and Captain of the Hook and Ladder and Hose. He also described how the mob carefully saved a painting of Queen Victoria in the Legislative Council, which still decorates the walls of Canada's Upper House, now the Senate. While they protected the Queen's portrait they stomped on a large painting of Papineau and destroyed it before leaving it to the flames that razed the building. The fire also destroyed some 20,000 books and manuscripts held by the library of United Canada. Acts of violence were perpetrated in the following days particularly aimed at those who had backed the Rebellion Losses Bill.

These events encouraged the advocates of annexation of Canada to the United States. In early October 1849, more than 300 people, including leading citizens like John Molson, John Redpath, and Antoine-Aimé Dorion, signed a manifesto in support of annexation in the belief that union with the United States would quickly solve all their problems. The United States was said to offer capital and skills, a vast market and cheaper goods, new railroads, increased prices for wood from Canada, and a straight-forward government that did not waste money. One might think that it was paradise. The annexation-ists made noise but little else, and soon another issue pushed their concerns aside. What city would host the new capital of United Canada after the troubles following the Rebellion Losses Bill had ruled out the idea of making Montreal the capital? Quite predictably, Governor Elgin chose Toronto.

While these events were occurring in the 1840s, Lower Canada was also undergoing major changes. The Catholic Church was gaining ground among the *Canadiens*, especially following the repression of the Patriotes in 1837 and 1838. A preaching tour of Lower Canada by Bishop Charles-Auguste de Forbin-Janson from France marked the beginning of Parish retreats. The revolutionary movements in Europe in 1848 were also an incentive for members of religious orders to take refuge in Quebec where they were welcomed by both Church authorities and the British colonial officials. This consolidated the revival of religious practice that had ebbed in the first half of the 19th century. Soon thereafter, the Jesuits returned, followed by the Clerics of Saint Viator, the Oblates, and the Congregation of the Sacred Cross. Religious orders for women were also established in Lower Canada, including the Sisters of the Sacred Heart and the Sisters of the Good Shepherd of Angers. New indigenous orders were also founded such as the Sisters of Providence, the Congregation of the Sisters of the Holy Names of Jesus and Mary, the Institut des soeurs de la Miséricorde, and the Sisters of Sainte-Anne. Religious organizations became the backbone of education and social services. Parish libraries were established to counter the threat of "bad books" and severe censorship was practised. Liberalism in whatever form became the arch enemy, including the budding Liberal Party, denounced for its "rougisme." Many members of the clergy likened the Liberal Party to the liberalism that had swept through France. Freedom of thought and of speech represented a threat to the Church.

The founding of the *Institut canadien* in December 1844 was a turning point in the intellectual life for many French Canadians. Jean-Baptiste-Éric Dorion, who participated in the creation of the organization, described its goals as follows: "A centre for emulation where every young man starting out in the world can draw inspiration of pure patriotism, learn by taking advantage of a community library, and grow accustomed to taking part in the deliberations of this tribune that is open to people of all classes and all conditions." By 1855, the *Institut Canadien* had 700 members who had access to a reading room with about one hundred newspapers and a library with approximately 4000 books, some of which were on the Index of forbidden books. The Catholic Church had proclaimed that reading such books was a mortal sin. At that time there were more than 60 such reading rooms available. The Montreal association became the bête noire of Bishop Ignace Bourget. The fact that many Liberals were members of the *Institut Canadien* made it a lightning rod for ecclesiastic rage until 1877 when Wilfrid Laurier drew the distinction between liberalism in Great Britain and the doctrinaire liberalism that had developed in France.

During the second half of the 1850s the population of Upper Canada grew to exceed that of Lower Canada. Equal representation for both had been touted as being fair when the Act of Union was imposed and Upper Canada was considerably less populated than Lower Canada. However, when the tables were turned it suddenly became a case of grave injustice. George Brown, founder of the *Globe* newspaper (now *The Globe and Mail*), championed the cause of "Rep by pop" or representation based on the population. This demand became a campaign theme in the 1857 general elections that pitted Liberals against Conservatives. In Lower Canada George-Étienne Cartier took over from Louis-Hyppolyte La Fontaine as leader of the French Canadians. Cartier formed a united front with John A. Macdonald, the Upper Canada leader of the Conservative Party. Political parties had to obtain a majority in both Upper and Lower Canada in order to govern and this resulted in short-lived governments. Between 1857 and 1864, six governments held power, the shortest lived being that of George Brown and Antoine-Aimé Dorion, which only lasted four days.

This instability forced political leaders to seek a lasting solution, and people were increasingly drawn to the idea of

uniting all the British colonies in North America. In July 1858
Alexander Tilloch Galt, the member for Sherbrooke, proposed a series of resolutions that would lead to the establishment of a federal union, since the existing legislative union
unfailingly led to gridlock. Galt believed that a general federation of the provinces of New Brunswick, Nova Scotia,
Newfoundland, and Prince Edward Island with Canada and
territories to the west was very desirable and that it would
enable them to advance both their common and different
interests. Each province was to maintain its particular institutions and its internal affairs. His proposal was not received
unanimously but it allowed opponents to stake out their positions clearly. For Joseph-Charles Taché, the central government's powers would emanate from the provinces. "The
federal pact," he wrote, "would be founded on the principle
of the permanent and unalterable delegation of powers by the
separate governments of the provinces to the general government in the form of distinct responsibilities established by
virtue of a written constitution."

Federating the British colonies in North America was
attractive for a number of reasons. Further development of
the railroads meant linking the centres of the colonies to
those on the Atlantic seaboard. Some Canadian politicians
also dreamed of playing an international role. In Great Britain
the proponents of a "Little England" fought to abandon all of
England's colonies gradually. Since the Crimean War had
broken out fewer British troops were stationed in Canada,
whereas Civil War was raging in the United States as of 1861
and that raised the question of how to defend Canada. When
a bill to reform the colonial militia was presented in 1862, the
fault lines between French and English speakers opened once
again. Members from Upper Canada voted unanimously for
the proposed reform, whereas both Liberal and Conservative

members from Lower Canada voted against it. Cartier lost his majority in the House while Macdonald maintained his majority and so the Cartier-Macdonald government was forced to resign. Many among the English reproached the French Canadians for their lukewarm, not to say disloyal, attitude towards defence of the land. In the eyes of *The Morning Chronicle* in Quebec City, the consequences were devastating. The May 21 editorial stated: "It is a declaration on the part of the thirty-seven Lower Canada constituencies, that the colony will not discharge its duty to the Crown in the vital matter of defence; and the world is bound to estimate it. No amount of lip-loyalty will suffice to obliterate this impression. A French Canadian majority have refused to pay a few dollars, and to perform slight service, as the price of continued British connection; and their actions must so stand before the world." *The Times* of London went even further suggesting that the very links between the colony and the mother country should be called into question.

A new version of the militia bill was proposed in 1863 while Civil War was raging in the United States and raising fears of invasion, partly because Britain had sided with the Confederacy and English-speaking Montreal had become a haven for Confederacy supporters and spies. In fact, John Willkes Booth, the man who assassinated President Abraham Lincoln, stayed in Montreal in 1864 just weeks before he killed Lincoln. After the Civil War, the leader of the Confederacy Jefferson Davis stayed in Montreal in the home of an upstanding English Montrealer by the name of John Lovell after being freed on bond pending trial in Richmond.

The militia bill was finally adopted and it received Royal Sanction on October 15. It stipulated that all men between 18 and 60 were members of the militia. Some categories of citizens were exempted from military service. These included judges, members of the clergy, college and university teachers and professors as well as elementary school teachers belonging to religious orders. As could be predicted, members of parliament were also exempted, along with doctors, surgeons, postmasters, active seamen, railroad employees, elementary school teachers, and so on. Interestingly enough, conscientious objectors could not be forced to take up arms.

Government instability continued to plague Parliament and exasperated George Brown to the point that he proposed a coalition government. His resolution was adopted on May 19, 1864, a milestone in the march towards a new Constitution. Quebec City was hosting the Government of United Canada at that time. It was learned that the Atlantic colonies were to meet early in September that year to discuss the possibility of uniting. The Canadian authorities decided to attend the meeting after receiving an invitation to be observers. They managed to convince the representatives from Newfoundland, Prince Edward Island, Nova Scotia, and New Brunswick that a truly efficient union could not be established without the participation of United Canada. It was agreed that another meeting would be held in Quebec City in October.

The decisions reached at the Quebec Conference that opened on October 10, 1864 became the basis of a bill aimed at uniting the colonies interested in doing so. The 33 representatives of the British colonies in North America would be called the "Fathers of Confederation," even though some of those present failed to convince their respective governments to join. One major issue at stake was to determine whether it would be a legislative or a federative union while another involved the representation of each colony within the central government. The Atlantic colonies were determined to obtain the construction of a railroad linking the colonies. The head of the line was to be the port of St. John, New Brunswick, or Halifax, Nova Scotia. It was agreed each colony's legislature had to approve the 72 resolutions adopted at the conference.

Before the bill was studied in the House, Antoine-Aimé Dorion, Leader of the Liberal Party of Lower Canada, demanded that the bill be put to a vote in a referendum. He believed that the proposed union "could only delay the progress and prosperity of the country" and concluded saying, "I reject it because I believe it to be contrary to the interest of the entire province and above all disastrous for Lower Canada." During the parliamentary debate that began in March 1865, Macdonald asserted that in his opinion a legislative union would be the best formula but the attitude of the French-speaking population of Canada East, as Lower Canada was then called, represented a major obstacle. Cartier in turn considered that no other project than the federal system would be possible. "Some parties pretended that it was impossible to carry out Federation, on account of the differences of races and religions. Those who took this view of the question were in error. It was just the reverse. It was precisely on account of the variety of races, local interests, that the Federation system ought to be resorted to, and would be found to work well."

A majority of the members from Canada, 91 of the 124 members, voted in favour of the resolutions emanating from the Quebec Conference and they were adopted. Historian Jean-Paul Bernard analysed the vote and concluded that "of the 62 members from Lower Canada, 37 voted for Confederation, while 25 opposed it. A finer analysis however showed that the bill received the support of only 27 French Canadian members out of 49." After refining the analysis even further, he concluded that in fact 25 French-speaking members voted in favour of the bill and 24 voted against it. Mildly put, it passed with a very slim majority.

For the bill to be implemented, the Parliament in London
had to adopt a specific act, but union of the colonies was high
on the agenda when a new threat appeared. Irish immigrants
to the United States had formed a movement known as the
Fenians and were plotting to take over the two Canadas and
use them to negotiate the independence of Ireland. To counter
the threat, thousands of militiamen in Quebec City and
Montreal took up arms. The Government of Canada was also
able to mobilize some 1500 Iroquois braves who were prepared
to fight to defend the land.

Although the Fenian raids sparked a reaction in some
quarters, more people were worried about the fate of the
English-speaking minority in Lower Canada who feared they
were being sacrificed to the French-speaking majority. To
appease them, some politicians pointed out that even if the
Legislative Assembly were to comprise a majority of French-
speaking members, the members of the Legislative Council
appointed by the Crown would champion the minority. In
addition, certain electoral ridings with a majority of English-
speaking voters could not be abolished nor have their boundaries modified without the approval of their representatives.
In education, a specific clause ensured that Protestant schools,
undoubtedly English, would continue to exist. In a spirit of
equity, Catholic schools in Upper Canada were to enjoy the
same rights. George-Étienne Cartier became the champion of "bonne entente" or good understanding. Speaking at
a banquet in Montreal at the end of October in 1866, he
declared that "French Canadians should not fear the English.
After all, they are not that frightening. Let us rather admire
their energy and their perseverance. Let's imitate them. To be
an excellent French Canadian, one should have all the qualities of our race and the best qualities of the English
Canadians."

At Westminster, the bill was first studied by the House of Lords who approved it on February 26, 1867. The bill was scarcely noticed in the House of Commons where the Honourable Members were more concerned by a bill to tax hunting dogs! John A. Macdonald witnessed the debate, or absence thereof, and wrote that the Union was treated as though it were an association of two or three parishes. On March 29, Queen Victoria granted Royal Sanction to the British North America Act and it came into force on July 1, 1867.

The four colonies, Lower Canada, Upper Canada, New Brunswick, and Nova Scotia, united to form the new Dominion of Canada, a name approved by the Queen. The new Constitution established a federal government and provincial governments. The federal government had jurisdiction over everything that concerned more than one province. It had the power to "make laws for the peace, order, and good Government of Canada in relation to all Matters not coming within the Classes of Subjects by this Act assigned exclusively to the Legislatures of the Provinces," which was the opposite of what was stipulated in the Constitution of the United States where anything that does not fall under federal government jurisdiction automatically became state responsibility.

In Canada the federal government was responsible for regulation of shipping and trade, postal service, the military and the navy, navigation, all monetary-system issues, banks, weights and measures, interest, patents and copyrights, naturalization of the foreign born, penitentiaries and criminal law, "Indians and land reserved for the Indians," as well as marriage and divorce. The powers assigned to the provinces on the other hand were limited. The provinces were responsible for celebrating marriages, civil rights, prisons, hospitals, administration and sale of provincially owned public lands, municipal institutions, "Generally all Matters of a merely local or private Nature in the Province." In short, the provinces had very little power. Section 93 of the Constitution nonetheless specified that education was the exclusive responsibility of the provinces. On the question of language, official bilingualism was limited to the "Records and Journals" of the houses of legislature of Canada and Quebec. English or French could be used in those two Parliaments and before the courts established by the federal government or by the Province of Quebec. In addition acts of the Parliament of Canada and the Quebec Legislature had to be printed and published in both languages.

Immigration and agriculture were two areas where power was to be shared. Since the maritime provinces were not interested in joining Canada unless an inter-colonial railroad was built, a specific section of the Constitution addressed the issue.

In Ottawa, during the Saint-Jean-Baptiste celebrations on June 24, 1867, George-Étienne Cartier waxed triumphant: "Confederation is a tree whose branches extend in different directions, all of which are firmly attached to the trunk. We French-Canadians are one of those branches. It is for us to understand this, and to work for the common good. Patriotism in its true sense is that which does not fight with a spirit of fanaticism, but which, while safeguarding what it cherishes, wishes that his neighbour should be no more molested than himself. This tolerance is indispensable. It was by it that we cooperated in this great work in which it was agreeable to our ambition to claim a part of honour." For Canada and for Quebec, a new era had just begun.

On April 25, 1849, English-speaking rioters opposed to the Rebellion Losses Bill set fire to the Parliament of United Canada located in the Marché Sainte-Anne at Place d'Youville in Old Montreal. Ironically, the man who started the fire, Alfred Perry, was a volunteer fireman and captain of the fire squad known as the Hook and Ladder and Hose.

CHAPTER 8

A Province Unlike the Others

Even though Confederation had become a fact the Liberal Party in Quebec continued to denounce it. Liberal leader Antoine-Aimé Dorion described the apprehended catastrophe in six short points: "1) Confederation is a loathsome act because the French language will be banned and our religion threatened; 2) It will necessitate additional expenditures and direct taxing; 3) It will bring on conscription and military enrolment; 4) It will lead to enormous spending on fortifications and on the inter-colonial railroad; 5) It will ruin industry and the workers; 6) It will put the Americans against us."

The Catholic episcopate was totally opposed to the Liberal leader's position believing that once Confederation had been officially established Catholics had no right opposing it. Some bishops issued writs reminding their churchgoers of their duty to obey. Thomas Cook, Bishop of Trois-Rivières, did not mince his words in his writ issued in French: "Nothing allows us to believe that 'Confederation' is an act of treason. It was discussed long enough, studied scrupulously by the most devoted and enlightened men of all provinces in order to eliminate any doubts about it. [...] Now that the bill has been sanctioned by the Imperial government and has become the fundamental law of the country, we must remember that our duty as Catholics is to put an end to all discussion about it.

[...] In all consciousness, my very dear brothers, and as Catholics and sincere friends of order, union, and peace, inasmuch as you have the strength and through your good will, you shall favour the smooth enforcement of the Constitution that will soon be inaugurated."

Some priests used their privileged position to preach to parishioners against voting for the Liberal Party calling it a mortal sin to do so. Since voting was not secret, it was easy for them to know who would go to hell if ever they died without confessing their sins! Despite all the finger-wagging sermons, Liberal candidates won the elections in 13 ridings, which meant that out of the 65 members elected to the House of Commons in Quebec, 52 were Conservatives. The provincial results were much the same. Since people were allowed to hold seats in both the House of Commons and the Quebec Legislative Assembly, some candidates were elected to both. This obviously complicated the task of convening the members of parliament.

The first session of the first Parliament in Quebec began on December 28, 1867 when the Lieutenant Governor gave the Throne Speech, first in French and then in English. This was an innovation since under the preceding Constitution English had precedence. Even though 75 percent of the population spoke French, the language issue worried many in Quebec. For example, Louis-François Laflèche, Bishop Coadjutor of Trois-Rivières marked the feast of Saint-Jean-Baptiste with a sermon in Ottawa on June 25, 1866, in which he stated that bilingualism represented a threat for French speakers. "The heaviest tax that the conquest has imposed on us is the necessity to learn English. Let us pay that tax loyally, but only what is necessary. Our tongue must always come first. We must hold to speaking the number one tongue of Europe. And let us fortify in our own house this powerful national bond."

The future of the French language and Catholicism was cause for concern also because thousands of French Canadians were emigrating to New England and draining Quebec of its population. The end of the Civil War in the United States spurred the migratory movement even more. In 1860 the Franco-American population was just upwards of 37,000. Twenty years later some 208,000 French Canadians were living in north-eastern United States and establishing "Little Canadas" centred on "national" parishes in which religious services were provided in French. Many of these parishes also provided schooling in French. Some leaders in the Catholic Church in the United States resolved to take action to assimilate these French Canadians and make them into good English-speaking American Catholics.

French Canadian presence in New England even became a political hot potato. Immigrants from Quebec were targeted by much of the media because of their desire to maintain their language and religion in the United States as well as their links with their homeland of Quebec. An editorial in *The New York Times* on June 6, 1892 provides a striking example of the prejudice they encountered. "It is said that there are more French-Canadians in New-England than there are in Canada. There are 400,000 in round numbers in New-England at this time, and in five of its principal cities they have the balance of power to-day. The Irish-American population is still larger, and it probably had the balance of power in more places, but to-day the second and third generations of the Irish-Americans are so nearly assimilated to the native population in political and social life that neither their religion nor its adjunct, the parochial school, is able to keep them out of the strong currents of American life. With the French Canadians this is not the case. Mr. Francis Parkman has ably pointed out their singular tenacity as a race and their extreme devotion to their religion, and their transplantation to the manufacturing centres and the rural districts in New-England means that Quebec is transferred bodily to Manchester and Fall River and Lowell. [...] It is next to impossible to penetrate this mass of protected and secluded humanity with modern ideas [...] No other people, except the Indians, are so persistent in repeating themselves. Where they halt they stay, and where they stay they multiply and cover the earth." The editorial then cited an historian who saw the French Canadian migration from Quebec as "part of priestly scheme now fervently fostered in Canada for the purpose of bringing New-England under the control of the Roman Catholic faith. He [the historian] points out that this is the avowed purpose of the secret society to which every adult French Canadian belongs." The New York Times proposed that the solution was "to compel the use of the English language in all the schools of American citizens."

This migration from Quebec also marked the future president of the United States Franklyn Delano Roosevelt who grew up in New York and New England in the 1880s and 1890s. In a 1942 letter to Canadian Prime Minister William Lyon Mackenzie King just after the conscription or military draft crisis, President Roosevelt suggested that Canada and United States "do some planning, perhaps unwritten planning, which need not even be a public policy by which we can hasten the objective of assimilating the New England French Canadians and Canada's French Canadians in the whole of our respective bodies politic. [...] Wider opportunities can probably be given to them in other parts of Canada and the US; and at the same time, certain opportunities can probably be given to non-French Canadian stock to mingle more greatly with them in their own centers."

The French Canadian experience in New England left a permanent imprint particularly on American and world literature. Jack Kerouac, who was born in Lowell Massachusetts in 1922 and only learned English at the age of six, constantly referred to his ancestors, the Plains of Abraham, and what he described in *Visions of Gerard* as the place "the French came when they came to the New World, the hardness of the Indians they must have embrothered to be able to settle and have them as conspirators in the rebellion against contrarious potent churly England." The migration of so many people to New England was an enormous loss for Quebec, but also for Canada since many could have been encouraged to go west and thus respond to Canada's needs for settlers.

* * *

Religious leaders in Quebec took a totally different tack from that of the Liberals of the time. Believing the Church to be above the State and its overseer, some bishops, priests, and laypeople attempted to influence the elections and avoid a Liberal victory. The "Catholic Program" made public in 1871 provided the following instructions: "It cannot be denied that politics is closely related to religion, and separation of the Church and the State is an absurd and impious doctrine. [...] Catholic voters must demand first and foremost that all Catholic candidates fully embrace the Roman Catholic doctrine as regards religion, politics, and social and economic affairs." Certain priests exerted "undue pressure" on their parishes to make them vote Conservative. The courts occasionally even cancelled some elections because voters had been exposed to "undue influence."

The Conservatives at both the provincial and federal levels were by no means beyond suspicion. In Quebec, corruption sullied the 1872 federal election campaign. John A. Macdonald's Government was building a railroad to link Montreal to

British Columbia, which had become a Canadian province a year earlier, and two financial groups were interested in the project. In an aim to influence the government and win the contract, one group gave the Conservatives $300,000 to help them get elected. Cabinet ministers John A. Macdonald, George-Étienne Cartier, and Hector Langevin received large kickbacks. The "Pacific Scandal" as it became known brought the Conservatives down and put power in the hands of the Liberals for a short time.

The Federal Parliament passed a law establishing the secret ballot in 1874. One year later the Government of Quebec followed suit despite opposition from some members. Future Premier Joseph-Adolphe Chapleau opposed the measure for moral and ethical reasons. "The secret ballot will not prevent corruption; on the contrary, the shame of being corrupted disappears when all is done secretly. [...] It is said that the secret ballot will protect people from having to vote against their convictions out of respect for others, however convictions that conflict with public opinion cannot be honest in politics."

The first Quebec general elections with a secret ballot were held on July 7, 1875. Wilfrid Laurier, who was gaining strength in the Liberal Party, endeavoured to clarify his party's position. During the campaign he declared: "We are liberal like those who are liberal in England; we are liberals like O'Connell! He is a leader for us, a man that so valiantly defended religion in the English Parliament; that is where we draw our doctrine and not from the so-called liberals who seek to impose their ideas in violence and loss of blood!" Two years later the future Prime Minister of Canada drove his point further home in the hope of putting an end to the debate on radical Rouge liberalism once and for all. "I know and I say that Catholic liberalism is not political liberalism. If it were true that Catholic censure of

Catholic liberalism were to apply to political liberalism, this fact would constitute for us, who are of French extraction and who are Catholic by religion, a situation with both strange and painful consequences. Indeed, we French Canadians are a conquered race. It is a sad fact but a true fact. However, although we may be a conquered race, we have also made a conquest, namely the conquest of freedom. We are a free people; we are a minority, but all our rights, all our privileges have been preserved. Now what cause has allowed us to be free. It is the constitution that was conquered for us by our forefathers, and that we enjoy today. [...] The priest who speaks and preaches as he sees fit has every right to do so. This right will never be challenged by a Canadian liberal. [...] The policy of the Liberal Party is to protect the institutions, to defend and promote them and, under the auspices of these institutions, develop the inherent resources of our country. That is what the Liberal Party stands for. It has no other policy." It would take time however for his adversaries to stop seeing Liberals as anything less than the devil incarnate.

The political arena had by no means a monopoly on problems, conflict, and tension. A serious economic crisis whose repercussions were felt for years struck both Quebec and Canada in 1873. Although the majority of the population lived in rural areas, migration to the cities was on the rise. With its factories and plants, Montreal was like a magnet for people from throughout Quebec and elsewhere in the world. In 1861 Montreal had a population of 90,000. Twenty years later, the population had jumped to 140,000, made up of 78,000 French Canadians, 29,000 people from Ireland, and 33,000 English Canadians. Rapid urbanization was accompanied by impoverishment among certain sectors of the population. Workers began to organize mutual organizations, which were forerunners to modern trade unions, and to formulate demands.

Shipwrights, longshoremen, and construction workers were among the first to organize. Wildcat strikes occurred and quite often ended up in violence and, in some cases, in death.

As the 19th century drew to an end, Quebec adjusted to all the currents that influenced the other Canadian provinces, United States, and Europe. In 1880 when the Government of Quebec had difficulty borrowing money to build railroads, it managed to obtain thousands of dollars on the French financial market. This led to the creation of the land and mortgage bank known as the Crédit foncier franco-canadien. For many people in France, it was the chance to rediscover a long-lost colony that delighted newspapers in Paris. "Lower Canada has remained so much a French province; it has maintained the mores, customs, and the language of the former inhabitants of New France that we can safely say that its current inhabitants are like fellow countrymen living overseas."

Rapprochement with France was not limited to the world of finance and cultural ties also gained strength. In December 1880, despite grave warnings issued by Bishop Bourget, Sarah Bernhardt triumphed as she arrived in Montreal and even more so when she premiered, despite the presence of the Marquis of Lorne, Governor of Canada, who was also Queen Victoria's nephew. Sarah Bernhardt's arrival in Montreal was a harbinger of General Charles de Gaulle's visit 87 years later. "This sound," she wrote in her memoirs, "soon resolved itself into music—and it was in the midst of a formidable 'Hurrah! Vive la France!' shouted by ten thousand throats strengthened by an orchestra playing the 'Marseillaise' with frenzied fury that we made our entry into Montreal." About the premiere, she wrote: "The house was noisy and quivering. Through an opening in the curtain I gazed on the composition of this assembly. All of a sudden a silence came over it without any outward reason for it, and the 'Marseillaise' was sung by three hundred warm young male voices. With a courtesy full of grandeur the Governor stood up at the first notes of our national anthem. The whole house was on its feet in a second, and the magnificent anthem echoed in our hearts like a call from the mother country. I do not believe I ever heard the 'Marseillaise' sung with keener emotion and unanimity. As soon as it was over the plaudits of the crowd broke out three times; then, upon a sharp gesture from the Governor, the band played 'God Save the Queen'. [...] The Marquis of Lorne thus smothered its last echo [the Marseillaise] beneath the English National Anthem."

The year 1880 also saw Calixa Lavallée, "Canada's national musician," compose the music for a patriotic poem written by Basile Routhier that was to be played for major festivities marking the Saint-Jean Baptiste Day in Quebec City on June 24, 1880. What was called the "chant national des Canadiens français" has since become Ô Canada, Canada's National Anthem. The occasion was the "Congrès national des Canadiens français," or French Canadian National Convention, attended by hundreds of French Canadians who made the pilgrimage to Quebec City from throughout North America. Moreover, the dozens of Acadians who attended that convention convened a similar convention of Acadians a year later followed by another in 1884 at which the Acadian flag was adopted. Bearing witness to the rapprochement with France, the Acadian flag was a French tricolour with a yellow star on the top left corner.

A very loud and rowdy crowd demonstrated in indignation in November 1885. Indeed, Canada then experienced its first major political crisis. Between 25,000 and 50,000 demonstrators assembled at the Champ de Mars in Montreal, on November 22, 1885, to hear orators denounce the hanging of Louis Riel and the consequences of the hanging. The crowd estimates differed depending on the language of the media. In English there were about 25,000 people, in French, 50,000. A few days earlier in Regina the leader of the Métis rebels had been hanged even though doctors had demonstrated that Louis Riel's mental health was disturbed. After all, Prime Minister John A. Macdonald had spoken bluntly and brutally about Riel. "He shall hang though every dog in Quebec bark in his favour." And he did hang!

Louis Riel was a Métis whose mother's family hailed from Maskinongé, in Quebec, and whose father was a Métis born in the west, the child of a French Déné woman and a Quebec born man. He had already been convicted in 1870 for leading the Métis revolt against surveyors who were dividing up the land the Canadian Government had bought a year earlier from the Hudson's Bay Company. As had been the case with the seigneurial system, the Métis had divided their land unofficially in long strips of land so that more people would have frontage on the lakes and rivers.

History repeated itself in Saskatchewan in the 1880s. A delegation of Métis sought out Riel in Montana where he was working as a teacher. They hoped to convince him to lead their protest movement. Many First Nations also took part. With the blessing of Bishop Ignace Bourget, some French Canadians joined the forces of order sent to crush the rebellion. The Métis and the First Nations were defeated and their leader Louis Riel was tried before an entirely English-speaking jury. He was sentenced to death and was hanged on Friday, November 16, 1885 despite protest from the French-speaking population of Canada. On the other hand an equally vociferous English-speaking population in Canada cried out for exemplary punishment for Riel. The Toronto newspaper *The Mail* wrote that the French Canadians should rest assured that, rather than live under their yoke, Ontario would be willing to break the ties of Confederation, recreate the original entities, and see the dream of a united Canada disappear forever. Speaking as "Britons," *The Mail* claimed that the fight for the conquest should go on and that Lower Canada should understand that this time there would be no Treaty of 1763, perceived to be a capitulation. The victors would not capitulate the next time, and the French Canadian people could expect to lose everything, their wealth and happiness for once and for all.

The news of Riel's hanging reached Quebec and set off demonstrations and protests. The new Montreal daily *La Presse* even invoked the possibility of Quebec becoming independent and wrote, "Riel is not only paying for demanding rights for his fellow countrymen; he is above all paying for the crime of belonging to our race." For a journalist with *Le Canadien* in Quebec City, "Blood is a poor bond and, if Confederation has no other bond, the wind that can overturn it is not far on the horizon." Lodges of the Orange Order in Ontario, known to be bitterly anti-French, voted resolutions congratulating John A. Macdonald, who was also a member of the Orange Order, and the Conservative Government for hanging Riel.

Political leaders in Quebec began to declare that no longer would there be Liberals and Conservatives, but rather the National Party and the hangman's noose party. Honoré Mercier, who was philosophically a liberal, channelled this dissatisfaction when he established the Parti National with the number one declared mission of defending the interests of French Canadians, but Wilfrid Laurier considered that a party with that approach would only harm the situation for French Canadians. In summer 1886, as the Quebec election campaign stirred up interest and passion, leaders from among the working masses in Montreal ran "working class candidates" for the first time. Quebec voted on October 14 and gave power to Honoré Mercier and his Parti National.

The new Premier of Quebec formed a common front with Ontario Premier Oliver Mowat to demand more powers for the provinces. They had rallied around the slogan of provincial autonomy and called the first interprovincial conference held in Quebec City in fall 1887. One resolution demanded that the provinces have the right to appoint half of the senators to the Upper House.

While that first interprovincial conference was sitting, the Royal Commission on the Relations of Labour and Capital began investigating the conditions of women and children at work. The report tabled in April 1889 revealed that girls and boys under 12 were working in cigar factories. The system of fines that prevailed meant that rowdy children would end up owing the boss money after a 60-hour work week. The commissioners recommended a law to limit the work week for women and children to 54 hours a week and 10 hours a day.

One of the first organized trade unions, the Knights of Labour from the United States, recruited many members in Quebec. Since the organization required that their talks and decisions remain secret, it was denounced by the Catholic clergy who forbade Catholics to join. The issue was referred to Rome where, in mid-August 1887, Pope Leon XIII decreed that there were no grounds for censuring such activity. Cardinal Elzéar-Alexandre Taschereau half deferred to the Vatican by tempering his previous order in a letter to the members of the clergy the following January. "For those who consult you, on my behalf, you will say that I strongly advise all Catholics in the Archdiocese of Quebec to avoid joining this society that is dangerous, to say the least, and to leave it as soon as possible if they are already members." The Knights of Labour lost ground to the Trades and Labour Congress of Canada, founded in 1883.

As the crisis provoked by the hanging of Louis Riel gradually died down towards the end of the 1880s, a new bone of contention arose when the Mercier government decided to settle the question of the Jesuits' property. When New France had capitulated in 1760 the Jesuits were prohibited from recruiting new members. At the time they had a number of seigneuries. The last Jesuit passed away in March 1800 and the government took over all Jesuit properties. For several decades thereafter debate continued on how the property should be used. Following broad consultations, Premier Honoré Mercier decided to settle the issue. The Jesuits themselves estimated that the property was worth $2 million, but Mercier offered them only $400,000. This amount was to be shared by the religious order, schools, and church dioceses. In order to appease the English-speaking population, $60,000 was earmarked for various Protestant and dissident universities and schools in Quebec. The Pope was invited to approve the settlement.

Some members of Parliament in Ottawa demanded that the Federal Government declare the Jesuits' Estates Act unconstitutional, but John A. Macdonald refused to go along. Race became the rallying cry once again. The Mayor of Toronto, Edward F. Clarke, was one of the first to use it on April 25, 1889. He claimed that French Canadians wanted to crush the English, that they wished to reconquer by intrigue that which they had lost due to the strength of English guns. He railed against the autocratic domination of Quebec, and their attempts to invade Ontario, which foretold their desire to become masters in the land. Fortunately, calmer heads ended up prevailing among the English-speaking population. Sparks flew again a few months later when the Equal Rights

Association was founded in Toronto with the goal of pro-
tecting the country against invasive French and aggressive
Catholicism. Honoré Mercier and Wilfrid Laurier, who was
then Leader of the Liberal Party of Canada, continually called
for a return of good understanding or *bonne entente*. In the
United States some Americans perceived that the French
Canadians were a threat to their country. On November 17,
1889, *The New York Times* echoed English Canadian suspicion. "The anti-Jesuit agitation promises to be prolonged. It
is learned that Premier Mercier of Quebec had an ulterior
object in view when he incorporated the Jesuits and paid them
indemnity for the surrender of all rights to their confiscated
estates. He proposes taking action against the Dominion
Government for the recovery of the Champ de Mars, or military parade ground, in Montreal. This property was included
in the confiscated Jesuit property, and instead of being applied
to educational purposes was reserved for the use of imperial
troops."

The measures taken to put an end to bilingualism both in
Manitoba and the North-western Territories did nothing to
calm things down. The Equal Rights Association was also
behind the fight to prohibit French. In Manitoba the law that
abolished separate schools, which were both Catholic and
French, and prohibited the official use of French came into
force on May 1, 1890.

The long reign of the Conservative Party was drawing to
an end in both Ottawa and at the provincial level. Ministers
embroiled in scandals weakened the party and many people
were demanding change. John A. Macdonald died in 1891
and, over the following five years, four different Prime
Ministers led government. General elections were held on
June 23, 1896, and Wilfrid Laurier was swept to power becoming the first French Canadian to hold the position of Prime

Minister of Canada. His party won 49 seats, leaving the Conservatives with a mere 16 seats even though the Catholic Church continued to back them. A year later the Liberal Party took power in Quebec City and held it non-stop until 1936.

Canada was still part of the British Empire and was not master of its own foreign policy. Thus, when Great Britain declared war it automatically declared war for Canada too. The question remained however as to the level of Canada's participation in wars that were declared by Great Britain. This theoretical question was put to the test in 1899 when London declared war on the Boers in South Africa. Diamond and gold had been discovered in the area and the British were adamant about having control. The British also had grand designs for Africa that included the never completed "Cape to Cairo" railway project so dear to the heart of Cecil Rhodes. While pressure was put on Prime Minister Laurier to send troops to fight alongside the British, pressure from other quarters favoured neutrality since the motives behind the military intervention in South Africa appeared dubious. An order in council dated October 13, 1899 stipulated that the federal government would pay for the equipment and transportation of a contingent of 1000 volunteer troops. When Henri Bourassa, who was Louis-Joseph Papineau's grandson, demanded that Wilfrid Laurier take into account the opinion of the French Canadians who, for the most part, were opposed to any Canadian participation in the war, the Prime Minister replied: "My dear Henri, the province of Quebec has no opinions, it only has feelings." The war in South Africa, known as the Boer War, lasted longer than expected, and some 7400 volunteers saw action.

Early in the 20th century, Quebec developed rapidly, spurred on by the advent of electricity and the modernization of plants and factories. The main areas of economic activity included the shoe industry, forestry, lumber and pulp and paper, dairy products, and the garment industry. Montreal had a population of 267,000 and was the undisputed centre of economic life in the country. The English-speaking population benefited most from the rapid economic growth, while the French-speaking people were largely relegated to low-paying manual labour.

Graduates of Quebec's classical colleges were generally streamed towards the religious orders, medicine, and law or notary studies. Science attracted very few young people and many were told that they had to carry the banner of French Catholic civilization and that French Canadians were simply not cut out for business. In a sermon on June 24, 1902 Catholic theologian Louis-Adolphe Paquet recalled that "our mission is less to handle capital than ideas; it consists less in firing up factory boilers than maintaining and caressing the sacred and illuminating fire of religion and thought."

In the 1840s Étienne Parent had bucked that current and later in the century Errol Bouchette rejected the idea that French-speaking population was unfit for business. "Our fellow countrymen in Quebec are no less apt for industry than the other races on this continent, and if they are well educated and guided they will obtain results that will astonish everybody and, above all, themselves." Alphonse Desjardins, who went from the army to a career in journalism and the civil service, knew how business worked and founded the first *"caisse populaire"* or credit union. Within a few short years many towns and villages developed similar institutions aimed to benefit small savers and investors. The nationalist rallying cry became, "We must take hold of industry."

French Canadian nationalism was on the rise at the end of the 19th century. The *"Ligue nationaliste canadienne,"* founded in March 1903, demanded that Canada, in its relations with

England, have the greatest political, economic, and military autonomy possible that would still be compatible with the colonial link, and that the Canadian provinces, in their relations with the federal government, have the greatest autonomy that would be compatible with the federal link. For the overall Confederation, the Ligue demanded adoption of an exclusively Canadian policy for the economic and intellectual development of the country. Not all French Canadians favoured the promotion of this type of Canadian nationalism. The journalist Jean-Paul Tardivel, who published the first separatist novel in 1895 entitled *Pour la patrie*, was among those opposed to Canadian nationalism. He set forth his ideas in his diary *La Vérité* on April 2, 1904. "Our nationalism is French Canadian nationalism. [...] What we want to blossom is French Canadian patriotism; for us 'we' and 'our people' mean French Canadians; for us, the mother country, is not exactly the province of Quebec, but French Canada; the nation that we wish to see founded on the date the divine providence chooses is the French Canadian nation."

The Catholic youth organization known as the *Association catholique de la jeunesse canadienne-française* (ACJC) was founded in Montreal in mid-March 1904. The ACGC thrived mainly among the youth in Quebec's classical colleges. It saw "the Canadian race as having a special mission to fulfil on the continent and [...] to do so it had to maintain its distinctive character in its relationship with the other races." The American historian Mason Wade wrote that this movement was the cradle of French Canadian nationalism in the 20th century and that the mix of religion and patriotism that it engendered permeated all of French Canadian life through the impassioned teaching that the young elite was receiving.

While some students were joining the nationalist movement, workers were organizing unions. The Catholic Church hierarchy endeavoured to counter the influence of the secular international trade unions by founding Catholic unions. The massive arrival of immigrants at the turn of the century was also perceived as a threat to both the French language and Catholicism. Between 1901 and 1910 Canada received 1,632,000 immigrants, with only 15,835 coming from France. Nationalist leaders called for people to join ranks and the first campaigns to buy locally were launched.

A need was also felt for higher business education. In March 1907, following lobbying efforts deployed by the recently founded Montreal Chamber of Commerce and despite opposition from leaders of the Catholic Church, the Quebec Legislative Assembly adopted a law creating the first business school in Canada, the École des Hautes Études Commerciales de Montréal, now known as HEC Montréal. This nondenominational French-language business school was unique in North America in that it was built along the European model of a specialized autonomous school with no specific links to a university. The new school was established near the Montreal business district, not far from St. James Street, in a new building architecturally inspired by the Petit Palais de Paris, which had been built for the Paris World Fair of 1900.

Henri Bourassa considered that Quebec was in dire need of an independent newspaper that would not be linked to any political party or movement. On January 10, 1910 the first issue of the daily Le Devoir appeared with the motto "Fais ce que doit" (Do thy duty). One of Le Devoir's first campaigns was to defend the French language which was threatened in Ontario and in the West. The Catholic bishop of London, Ontario, Michael Francis Fallon, called for the abolition of the French-language Catholic separate schools in Ontario. As was the case in New England, the Irish Catholic Church became a powerful factor in the assimilation of French-speaking people. Few however would dare raise their voices in protest. A climax was reached during the Eucharistic Congress of September 1910 in Montreal when the Pope's envoy, the Archbishop of Westminster Francis Bourne, openly proposed that the French-speaking Catholics abandon their language in the name of Catholicism. "It is only by bringing the English tongue to render service to the cause of truth that Canada can be made in the full sense a Catholic nation," insisted the august cleric. "Until the English language, English habits of thought, English literature—in a word the entire English mentality is brought into the service of the Catholic Church, the saving work of the Church is impeded and hampered." This upstanding archbishop, enthusiastically supporting the Empires headed by England and the Vatican, had dared to make this speech before a primarily French Canadian audience. The founder of the *Le Devoir* Henri Bourassa took it upon himself to make a stirring and much remembered reply to the obvious pleasure of the bishops in attendance.

The very many lodges of the Orange Order led the fight for the abolition of French schools just as they had mobilized against Louis Riel. They stated that the use of French in public schools in Ontario represented a serious threat to the integrity of the province as an English-speaking community. In June 1912 the Ontario Government adopted instructions that put their demand into effect. Instruction 17 stipulated that "As soon as the pupil enters the school he shall begin the study and the use of the English language. [...] Where necessary in the ease of French-speaking pupils, French may be used as the language of instruction and communication; but such use of French shall not be continued beyond Form 1. [...] And the provision for such instruction in French in the time table of the school shall be subject to the approval and direction of the Supervising Inspector and shall not in any day exceed one hour in each class-room." This new measure came into force in September 1913. Opposition in Quebec was unanimous, however nobody proposed similar measures be taken to limit the rights and privileges of the English-speaking minority.

This crisis boiled over at a time when war between Germany on the one hand and Great Britain and France on the other appeared imminent.

Louis Riel, c. 1870. Louis Riel was hanged on November 16, 1885 after being tried before an entirely English-speaking jury. Six days later, a massive demonstration was held at the Champ de mars in Montreal where the future Premier of Quebec, Honoré Mercier, declared that Riel was his brother. On the other hand, Prime Minister John A. Macdonald had declared that "He shall hang though every dog in Quebec bark in his favour." And he did hang.

CHAPTER 9

On All Fronts

When Germany declared war on Great Britain on August 4, 1914, Canada knew that it too was conscripted to fight and began recruiting its first volunteers. Some nationalists responded by claiming that the real battlefield was not in Europe, but in Ontario. Armand Lavergne, who held the seat in the Quebec Legislative Assembly for the riding of Montmagny located just east of Quebec City, made a startling declaration. "If they demand that we go and fight for England, we shall reply: Give us back our schools!" Lavergne was referring to the recently abolished French-language schools in Ontario.

In order to facilitate recruitment of troops for the trenches in Europe, city councils granted leave with full pay to all civil servants belonging to the militia and who would do active service in the war. The federal government adopted the Canadian Patriotic Fund Act to provide assistance to families of soldiers who lived in Canada and who were on active service with the Naval and Military Expeditionary Forces of the British Empire. Bishops of the ecclesiastical provinces of Ottawa, Montreal, and Quebec appealed for all Catholics to make generous donations to the Fund. They wrote to churchgoers saying, "Your donation will be shared. Half will be given to the Patriotic Fund managers for the purposes that are, or could be, legally set forth, and the other half will be shared in each diocese to those families who, because of forced unemployment or other reasons, are reduced to poverty, especially during the trying winter season."

A military training camp for volunteers was established at Valcartier, north of Quebec City, and in a very short time some 35,000 men were based there. Many boarded ships for England as early as the beginning of October 1914. A regiment in which French was to be the majority language was created so as to facilitate recruitment of French Canadians. The "Royal French Canadian" bore the number twenty-two, or vingt-deux, and later became known in English Canada as the "Vandoos." Despite the numbers of volunteers, people in certain English-speaking circles believed that too few French Canadians were willing to enrol. What's more, protest against Instruction 17 that abolished French-language education in Ontario was gaining ground. The Catholic youth organization, *l'Association catholique de la jeunesse canadienne-française*, launched a fund-raising campaign in support of the "wounded in Ontario," while the young Montreal daily *Le Devoir* took the lead in the language struggle. Founding publisher Henri Bourassa did not shy away from direct confrontation with the Government of Ontario and the Orange Order. "In the name of religion, freedom, and loyalty to the British flag, French Canadians are urged to go to and fight the Prussians in Europe. Are we going to allow the Prussians of Ontario impose their domination as masters, in the heart of the Canadian Confederation, and under the guidance of the British flag and institutions?" As a result of his leadership in the combined fight for French-language education and against compulsory military service, Henri Bourassa was tagged the internal public enemy number one in Canada. For example, when a history book used in schools in British Columbia in 1920 did not present Henri Bourassa as a traitor to the British Empire, the book was banned.

The Ontario school question was raised in the Quebec Legislative Assembly in January 1915. Two English-speaking members presented a motion deploring the divisions that appear to exist among the people of the province of Ontario with regards to bilingual schools. All members in attendance voted for the motion and a copy was sent to Bishop Fallon who was still convinced that Instruction 17 was a "just and fair solution." Some people urged Ottawa to intervene in the Ontario school issue even though education is the exclusive jurisdiction of the provinces.

The battles in Europe spread, wreaking death and destruction throughout. Pressure grew on the federal government to impose a military draft or conscription to raise more troops. During the first five months of 1916, according to the Canadian Annual Review, Quebec had only raised a quarter of the quota set, the Maritimes, half the quota, and Ontario, seven ninths. Only the western provinces had exceeded their quotas. Army recruiting officers doubled their efforts and became more aggressive, while recruitment committees were set up to attract volunteers using eye-catching ads. "Each soldier who enrols will receive $1.10 a day, his wife will receive an allowance of $20 a month as well as an allowance from the Patriotic Fund for her and her children."

Many French Canadians showed little interest in going to war in Europe, even though it was known that the Germans had begun to use lethal gases, but they were not alone. In his study on the First World War, historian Desmond Morton concluded that "Across Canada, most men of military age never volunteered. Those who lived on farms, were married, or had jobs or deep ancestral roots in the country were least likely to enlist. By no coincidence, the Maritimes ranked only a little ahead of Quebec in recruiting rates." Moreover, some nationalists notably led by journalist and pamphleteer Olivar

Asselin, believing that they had to defend France against Germany, valiantly campaigned in favour of a full war effort in Quebec.

The perceived general conduct of French Canadians in Quebec raised the ire of the Orangemen. Some were already apprehending the establishment of a French republic in the St. Lawrence Valley. One outspoken Orangeman declared that if it were necessary, some 250,000 Orangemen who were too old to fight overseas could nonetheless be mobilized within a month to destroy any attempt in the province of Quebec to found a republic.

In the early months of 1917 rumours about conscription were increasingly numerous and they were met by anti-conscription rallies in Montreal that attracted thousands. Compulsory military service was becoming necessary because for every new recruit two soldiers were falling on the battlefield. Prime Minister Borden tabled a bill in the House of Commons on June 11, 1917 calling for general mobilization. The Military Service Bill imposed compulsory service on all male British subjects aged 20 to 45 who lived in Canada or who had lived in the country since August 4, 1914. Debate on the Military Service Bill was acrimonious and only on August 28, 1917 did the Governor General, Duke of Connaught, grant Royal Sanction. Conscription obviously was the main issue in the federal election campaign in fall 1917. The other provinces provided a healthy majority to the coalition government led by Robert Borden, but Quebec bucked the current electing 62 Liberals, two Conservatives, and one Liberal-Unionist. The English-language media unleashed an anti-Quebec campaign and for the first time since Confederation not a single French Canadian was appointed to the new federal cabinet.

On December 21, 1917 the Liberal member of the Quebec Legislative Assembly for Lotbinière, Joseph-Napoleon

Francœur, tabled a motion that illustrated the climate that reigned in Canada. "That this House is of the opinion that the Province of Quebec would be disposed to accept the breakdown of the federal pact of 1867, if, in the other provinces, it is believed that this province is an obstacle to the union, progress, and development of Canada." The motion was debated shortly and then withdrawn. However, it represented the first manifestation of a negative separatism, namely that Quebec was ready to withdraw from the federation if the rest of Canada was not at ease. Premiers Louis-Alexandre Taschereau and Maurice Duplessis brandished the same threat a few years later. During the debate, a member from the island of Montreal was almost convinced that if Quebec were to withdraw from Canada, Montreal would form a new province.

When conscription was adopted, a vast hunt for deserters began, resulting in the death of four young Quebec men in Quebec City and the wounding of several soldiers among the Canadian troops. The wounded were mainly English-speaking soldiers from Toronto who had received orders to fire on demonstrators protesting against an arrest that they considered unjustified. The demonstrators had damaged some buildings before the army opened fire.

With the signing of the armistice on November 11, 1918 the First World War was over. As peace approached, the Spanish flu pandemic that left between 8000 and 14,000 dead in Quebec alone also subsided. Several months went by before the troops in Europe returned home. For some, homecoming celebrations were dry since sale of intoxicating beverages was prohibited as of May 1, 1919, except in certain specific cases. At that time intoxicating beverages included alcohol and all liquors, and all mixes of liquors, beverages, liquids, and edible solids with an alcohol content exceeding 2.5 percent. Under prohibition legislation, a referendum was to be called and the question was clear. "Is it your opinion that the sale of light beer, cider, and wine, as defined by law, should be allowed?" On April 10, 1919, YES supporters won the vote with a small majority. But seven ridings in which the English-speaking population was concentrated ended up with strict prohibition.

On July 9, 1920 Louis-Alexandre Taschereau was elected Premier of Quebec on a program that included promises to settle the questions of alcohol and public assistance. The following year he created the Quebec Liquor Commission that had absolute control over the sale of alcoholic beverages throughout Quebec. During the same year his government created a public assistance service. In the future one third of hospital fees for needy people would be paid by the Quebec government, another third by the municipality where the person lived, and the remainder by the public assistance institution. Some people saw this measure as the first step towards a government-run hospital system at a time when religious orders ran most hospitals.

Major changes took place in the Quebec society in the 1920s. The urban population outnumbered the rural population for the first time. The number of cars jumped from some 36,000 in 1920 to 140,800 just 10 years later. In the same period the number of trucks increased sevenfold. Electric utilities in 1920 served some 248,000 customers, but by 1926 they had more than 360,000 customers. While Quebec was the second richest province in Canada, control of the economy became the burning issue. In December 1921, in the review *L'Action française*, founded in 1917 and still published today as *L'Action nationale*, Abbey Lionel Groulx reported on a vast investigation of economic problems in Quebec and concluded: "A long three-century history, almost full possession of the land by a specific race, the profound imprint that this race has left on the land through its customs and original institutions, the special status that it has obtained in every Constitution since 1774, have made Quebec into a French State that must be recognized as such in theory and in practice. This fact must be raised to the summit so that it governs the economic order in our homeland, just as it is spontaneously recognized that it governs the other aspects of our lives." Such a statement made the next step of withdrawing Quebec from Canada very easy to take. Some nationalists took that step, but Lionel Groulx did not.

For most of the population, however, the burning economic issues came first. Armistice also ushered in a recession. Unemployment soared after being almost non-existent during the war. According to data provided by trade unions published in the *Workplace Gazette*, more than 16 percent of unionized workers were unemployed in 1921. Real unemployment rates were undoubtedly much higher since not all workers were unionized. The unemployment rate had dropped to 6.3 percent by November 1928, but exactly one year later it had shot up to 13.6 percent.

It would have been hard to foresee the tragedy that was about to strike in 1929. The cost of living had remained stable from 1921 on. In December of that year it cost $21.56 a week for a family of five to buy general foodstuffs and pay for fuel, lighting, and rent, based on average prices in 60 Canadian cities. For the same month in 1928 the same family would have paid only seven cents more a week.

Thousands of Quebecers invested money on the stock market, with many playing on margin. The value of most shares had doubled, tripled, or even quadrupled, making stock market fever contagious. Early in October 1929 the New York Stock Market began to falter and then crashed on Thursday 24 October. Shares in DuPont of Nemours that had been selling for $231, for example, were now being sold for a mere $22. Small-time speculators panicked and the situation became progressively more confused in the following weeks. Some shares would rise rapidly while others would bottom out completely. Slowly but surely Quebec settled in to the Great Depression along with the other countries in Europe and America. Many people were ruined and some committed suicide to avoid facing the disaster. Factories and plants laid off thousands of workers and unemployment became chronic, boosting Quebec's unemployment rate to a summit of 30.9 percent among unionized workers in December 1932.

When the Depression began, needy people could only count on assistance from charities or from family and friends. In summer 1930 the Quebec government and the City of Montreal provided a few hundred thousand dollars to help the hardest hit. In the following years public work projects were launched to combat unemployment but not everybody was able to find work and so the three levels of government established a direct social assistance system. The federal government, the provincial governments, and the municipalities were each to contribute a third. However, early in 1933 some thirty municipal or school corporations were put under public trusteeship. With bankruptcy knocking, federal civil servants underwent a 10-percent salary cut.

Social and political tensions heightened. "Foreigners" and women who were still working were targeted and accused of stealing jobs from honest fathers and providers. Action was taken to keep the unemployed off the island of Montreal. The Valcartier military base was transformed into a relief camp for unemployed bachelors who were expected to perform certain tasks in return for 20 cents a day. That amount soon earned them the moniker "Twenty Centers."

The early 1930s marked the appearance of a new strategy for countering unemployment in the cities and particularly in Montreal. It was known as "return to the land." The Quebec government and certain members of the clergy and nationalist organizations advocated migration to the Abitibi area in north-western Quebec where hundreds of plots of land were made available. The Taschereau government invested tens of thousands of dollars into making homesteaders out of city dwellers who knew absolutely nothing about working the land. The operation was a failure, but also because many of the lots granted were rocky and barren. The member of the Legislative Assembly for Abitibi, Hector Authier, wrote to the Montreal City Council to express his dismay about the operation. "Back to the land: Would you please tell your people in Montreal that Abitibi is neither a hospital nor an emergency shelter and that we have no charitable organizations like the Saint-Vincent-de-Paul. People here are charitable, but we've already had enough of your people. If everybody looks out for their own poor, things will be better."

Some nationalists were convinced that the solution to all the problems could be obtained through Quebec independence. Some university students founded a new organization known as the Jeune-Canada or Young Canada. On April 18, 1935 a member by the name of Paul Simard declared: "We must conquer our intellectual, political and economic independence at all cost. [...] Quebec must become a free state as soon as possible where the French Canadian nation will be absolutely master of its destiny. In the economic sphere, we must defeat all the foreign dispossessors. A spiritual resurrection of this nature can only be accomplished when everybody rallies behind a single banner, the banner of one leader." For these young people Lionel Groulx was the ideal leader. Two years later the Catholic canon and historian announced his colours in an address before the Congress of the French Language. "Whatever happens, we shall obtain our French

State. We shall have it and it will be young, strong, radiant, and a spiritual home and dynamic pole for all French America. We shall also have a French country, a country that will be able to wear its soul on its face." When the newly-elected Quebec Premier Maurice Duplessis criticized him and when Cardinal Rodrigue Villeneuve, who 14 years earlier had predicted the "willing or forceful break-up of Canada," echoed the premier, Lionel Groulx clarified his position. "I am not a separatist. When I talk about a French State, I am talking about a federative State. I remain in line with history. We did not enter Confederation in order to leave it, but to achieve fulfilment." For the nationalist leader, the future of Quebec lay within the federal framework inasmuch as possible, and if not possible, it would be outside the federation.

While some people were proposing independence as a solution to pull out of the Depression, others were in favour of a communist government. In order to put down the "communisses," as he called them, Duplessis pushed the infamous Padlock Law through the Legislative Assembly. The Padlock Law allowed the Quebec Provincial Police, now the Sûreté du Québec, to padlock doors of premises occupied by people suspected of being communists or communist sympathizers. The problem of course was that the law failed to define a "communist." On the other end of the political spectrum, fascist ideas were also developing. In February 1934 Adrien Arcand and some friends founded the *Parti national social chrétien*, also known as the Christian National Socialist Party, and openly showed support for Hitler and his doctrines. Arcand had begun publishing anti-Semitic material in two papers in 1930 with considerable financial help from the leader of the Conservative Party and future Prime Minister of Canada Richard Bennett. Support from the Conservatives would continue throughout the 1930s. When war was declared against Germany in September 1939, Arcand's party was outlawed and its leaders were interned.

A more mainstream position was held by another group of secular intellectuals who included Esdras Minville, Philippe Hamel, Anatole Vanier, and René Chaloult. Together with Jesuits from the school known as the *École sociale populaire*, they drafted a social revival program with the broad goal of reforming French Canadian society. They recommended establishing a farmers' loan system, allowances for needy mothers, a minimum wage, strict observance of Sunday, the return of mothers to their homes, regulation of purchasing in instalments, creation of a provincial economic council, and more.

The ideas in the Social Revival Program pleased some Liberal members of the Quebec Legislative Assembly who were dissatisfied with the policies of the Taschereau government, increasingly under attack for patronage and corruption. These members formed a group known as the *Action libérale nationale* (ALN) led by Paul Gouin. This group and the Quebec Conservative Party led by Maurice Duplessis effected a rapprochement as the Quebec elections to be held on November 25, 1935 approached. The Liberals remained in power winning 48 of the 90 seats up for grabs. Sixteen Conservatives were elected and 26 members of Paul Gouin's *Action libérale nationale*. During the following parliamentary session Duplessis hammered away at the Premier and several ministers on the dubious management of public accounts. Taschereau was forced to resign and was replaced by Adélard Godbout before new elections were called on August 17, 1936. The *Union nationale*, created by the merger of the Conservative Party and the ALN, swept to power with 76 of the 90 seats in the Legislative Assembly. The Liberal Party left power after having held it since 1897.

A new reign began, but it was interrupted for several years when the Liberals under Godbout won the election in October 1939, just one month after Canada entered the war against Germany. Duplessis, whom the banks had decided to boycott, called snap elections. Conscription became the major issue of the campaign. Liberal campaign speakers constantly reminded voters that the federal Conservatives had imposed compulsory military service during the First World War. Two days before Canada joined the war, Canada's Liberal Prime Minister, William Lyon Mackenzie King had solemnly sworn that "The present government believes conscription of men for overseas service will not be a necessary or effective step. No such conscription measure will be introduced by the present administration." Godbout's commitment was even more compelling. "I undertake, on my honour and weighing each and every word, to leave my party and even combat it if a single French Canadian, between now and the end of the war, is mobilized against his will under a Liberal government, and even under a provisional government in which our current ministers in Mr. King's cabinet are serving."

Fear that compulsory military service abroad would be imposed grew when the national registration campaign was announced. Already on June 18, 1940, four days after German troops had occupied Paris, Mackenzie King announced conscription for the entire Canadian territory, which would grow with time since the still independent Newfoundland and the Aleutian Islands were annexed for military purposes. All Canadian men and women aged 16 to 60 had to register between August 19 and 21. It was well known that bachelors would be the first to be conscripted and so young men and women raced to get married. Believing national registration was the first step towards full conscription, the mayor of Montreal Camilien Houde of Montreal recommended that people not show up for registration. He made the statement "off the record" to a reporter from *The Montreal Gazette*, but the Montreal daily printed his remarks under a screaming headline. That was enough to have the mayor of Canada's largest city, who was also a member of the Quebec Legislative Assembly, arrested and interned for four years at the Fredericton and Petawawa military camps!

Mackenzie King's promise not to implement conscription for overseas service became increasingly problematic. The Throne Speech on January 22, 1942 announced a cross-Canada plebiscite that, if approved, would relieve the federal government from the obligation to honour a promise it had made only to the people of Quebec. The Canada Defence League organized many rallies in Montreal that often degenerated into public brawls. The plebiscite was held on April 27 and people were asked: "Are you in favour of releasing the Government from any obligations arising out of any past commitments restricting the methods of raising men for military service?" The results were predictable. For Canada as a whole, 80 percent voted YES, whereas 70 percent of Quebecers voted NO. The Mackenzie King government introduced the conscription bill to the House of Commons shortly after the vote. Total conscription was only decreed, however, on November 23, 1944. For years thereafter, many Quebecers perceived the plebiscite to be the epitome of deceit since, to get elected, Mackenzie King had promised only to Quebec that conscription would not be imposed, but his government then invited all of Canada to use its majority to override the will of the people of Quebec.

Daily life for most people in Quebec was shaken up by the war. Censorship was applied to all newspapers and radio. Gas consumption was first controlled and then rationed. Butter, sugar, tea, coffee and many other goods could only be obtained upon presentation of ration coupons. The black market flour-ished and some got rich very quickly. Car owners were pro-hibited from lending each other tires or tubes and it was impossible to buy new tires. Many people thought that the authorities were using certain measures simply to create a war psychosis. For instance, the manufacture of teacups with two handles was prohibited, supposedly to save raw materials. Another emergency measure specified that buttons on suit sleeves had to be eliminated.

War or not, the first signs of a "Quiet Revolution" could be detected. The Godbout government adopted a number of measures that can be seen to have ushered in new times. Women finally earned the right to vote in Quebec elections in 1940. They had already been voting in federal elections since 1918. Quebec was the last province to grant women the right to vote. Leading members of the Church including Cardinal Villeneuve held that the women's suffrage would undermine marital authority. In the March 7, 1940 edition of the Quebec City-based Semaine religieuse, Cardinal Villeneuve defended the Church's position. "We are not in favour of political suffrage for women: 1) because it goes against the unity and hierarchy of the family; 2) because exercise of this right will expose women to all the passion and adventures of electoral politics; 3) because, in fact, it appears to us that the vast majority of women in this province do not wish to obtain the right to vote; 4) because the social, economic and hygiene reforms and other such reforms that are advanced to justify women's suffrage can also be obtained through the influence of women's organization outside the realm of politics. We believe to be expressing the feelings held by all bishops in the province." Women eligible to vote had to wait until the next general elections in 1944 before they could vote for the first time. The clergy also believed that the parents themselves had entrusted the Church with the mission of educating the young. Their opposition to compulsory education also explains why a law to that effect was only adopted in 1943. Under that law parents had to send their children aged 6 to 14 to school or be fined.

The following year the Godbout government nationalized the Montreal Light, Heat and Power Company and created the Quebec Hydroelectric Commission that later became known as Hydro-Quebec. Whereas labour relations under Duplessis's first government were extremely tense, they were much more harmonious under Godbout. Historian Jacques Rouillard summarized the measures adopted between 1939 and 1944 as follows: "During the short Liberal government the socially oriented legislation was generally well received by the trade unions. That was the case with the Superior Labour Council (1940), the Minimum Wage Act applied to all wage-earners (1940), the constitutional amendment enabling the establishment of Unemployment Insurance (1940), and the Act to establish an Economic Orientation Council (1943), [...] and the Labour Relations Act (1944)." The Godbout government did not have time to establish a universal health insurance plan. Some people believe that if Godbout had won the Quebec general elections on August 8, 1944, the momentous events that are known as the "Quiet Revolution" would have taken place before 1960. However, the return of Maurice Duplessis and the Union nationale meant that those types of reforms were put on a back burner.

Headlines in the Montreal daily La Presse on April 2, 1918. "Five civilians killed by soldiers in Quebec City." Large numbers of people—more than 15,000 some days—demonstrated regularly against the Military Service Bill or conscription during the First World War. Opposition in Quebec to participation in foreign wars in the name of the British Crown had begun during the Boer War in South Africa (1899-1902).

Lumberjacks rest at a bush camp in the 1930s. The forest industry had become extremely important to Quebec economy in the early part of the 20th century.

CHAPTER 10

A New Society Comes to Life

The end of the war brought the men and women who had taken part in one way or another back home. Their travels had given them another outlook on life and the world around them and broadened their horizons. The industry of war was also sputtering and women who had been working in the weapons industry bore the brunt of the factory closings. Fortunately, however, the residential construction boom that followed the war helped fill the void. What's more, people had tended to be thrifty during the war and thus had savings to buy new homes and appliances.

Quebec's population increased by 21.7 percent between 1941 and 1951. Those who had put off marrying during the war rushed to tie the knot and the baby boom began. In 1941 Quebec recorded some 91,000 births. In 1946, 113,500 babies were born and by 1951 births had reached 138,600 a year. More than a quarter of the people in Quebec were under 10 years old. This baby boom resulted both from families deciding to have more children and from more women deciding to have children.

The baby boom boosted the population of Quebec but massive immigration also contributed. The context of war had virtually shut down the ports to new citizens. After the war immigrants began to arrive from countries other than the traditional ones. The number of immigrants from the United

Kingdom and Ireland dropped while more and more people came from Spain, Portugal, and above all from Italy. Montreal continued to attract most of Quebec's new immigrants. Duplessis was back in power after the general elections of August 1944. Provincial autonomy was high on his government's political agenda. Returning from a federal-provincial conference in 1946, Duplessis declared: "The autonomy of the province, the rights of the province, therein lays the soul of a people, of the race, and nobody will be allowed to do it any harm. They are the rights and prerogatives that enable us to raise our children in the French language and in the Catholic religion. [...] We have a choice position in the Confederation. In numbers, we form a minority, but we are a majority because of our years on this land. The Province of Quebec demands the right to live and to ensure its survival." Some believed that Duplessis's provincial autonomy was an empty concept, just hot air.

Duplessis decided to give "his" province a flag, just as the other provinces had done. Some nationalists had already been campaigning for a flag for years. An order in council on January 21, 1948 officially made the fleur-de-lis Quebec's flag. It comprised a white cross and four white lilies on a blue background, a clear reminder of Quebec's roots in France. For one reporter with *The Montreal Gazette*, the flag was adopted mainly because of the looming Quebec elections.

The policies of the Union nationale combined with the prevailing political climate resulted in a divided population. Movies in Quebec were severely censored by a government agency. Communists and Jehovah's Witnesses were targeted for repression, and the Catholic clergy held pervasive power. Bishops in Quebec published a pastoral letter in which they deplored the immorality and immodesty that, in their eyes, had invaded Quebec. Two years later, artists and intellectuals denounced the climate of oppression that they felt pervaded Quebec. Signatories of the *Refus Global* or Total Refusal claimed that "The reign of hydra-headed fear has ended. In the wild hope of effacing its memory, I enumerate: fear of facing prejudice—fear of public opinion—of persecutions—of general disapproval; fear of being alone, without the God and the society which isolate you anyway; fear of oneself—of one's brother—of poverty; fear of the established order—or ridiculous justice; fear of new relationships; fear of the superrational; fear of necessities; fear of floodgates opening on one's faith in man—on the society of the future; fear of forces able to release transforming love; blue fear—red fear—white fear; links in our shackles." The manifesto had very little impact when it first appeared but it heralded the profound and sweeping change on the horizon.

Confrontation with workers was much more violent, particularly because the Duplessis government held the union movement in contempt. Premier Duplessis, who was also Attorney General, believed that some unions were infiltrated by communists. During the strike at the Montreal Cotton Limited works in Valleyfield, he declared: "My government will never tolerate the methods of communist propaganda which is even more dangerous for public health than is tuberculosis for an individual's health."

The strike that most marked the times was undoubtedly the Asbestos miners' strike in 1949. Although asbestosis seriously jeopardized their health, the miners focused their demands on wage increases at the Canadian Johns-Manville mine in the town of Asbestos south of Quebec City. The workers and the police were constantly clashing. The strike went on and on and steadily degenerated while strikers found themselves lacking the basic necessities. Campaigns were launched to support the strikers and provide them with food and clothing.

Members of the clergy joined in and Canon Lionel Groulx called for a national campaign in support of the strikers. "These strikers are not like other strikers. They are not only fighting for wages and food. They are fighting for their very life and that of their girls and boys who work in a murderous industry. [...] Time has come to call on support from the entire population. The whole province has the duty to put an end to this undeserved misery." The Archbishop of Montreal, Joseph Charbonneau, intervened directly in the strike. In his eyes, "the working class was the victim of a plot to crush it and when there is a plot to crush the working class, the Church has the duty to intervene." Premier Duplessis obviously took a very dim view of Monsignor Charbonneau's position and forced him to resign as Archbishop of Montreal. Monsignor Charbonneau ended his life in Victoria, British Columbia, where he was chaplain to the Sisters of Sainte-Anne.

The 1950s were marked by more strikes that often ended in violence. Duplessis believed that company bosses were expected to behave as good fathers, and workers were to be patient and even obedient. When the North Shore of the St. Lawrence was opened up for iron ore mining, many workers moved to the region to find work. In 1946 the Hollinger North Shore Exploration Company obtained an 80-year mining lease from the Quebec government for the North Shore region. The Iron Ore Company of Canada was incorporated—in the United States—in 1949. Six years later the Quebec North Shore company founded the town of Schefferville, located about 500 kilometres north of Sept-Îles, the nearest port on the Gulf of St. Lawrence. Duplessis was accused of selling the North Shore to mining companies for the meagre sum of one cent per ton of iron ore. The other clauses in the mining rights lease that guaranteed substantial income for the government were often forgotten.

Duplessis's attitude gave rise to many bitter editorials in the Montreal daily *Le Devoir*, which became the outspoken advocate of those opposed to the Quebec government. In 1950 another publication was founded that bolstered opposition to Duplessis. The review *Cité libre* included among its founding members Gérard Pelletier and Pierre Elliott Trudeau. Although *Cité libre* had a limited print run, it became quite influential among Quebec intellectuals. In its second issue, a contributor wrote: "Catholicism is not proposed or taught (in Quebec), but rather imposed, meted out, inflicted upon people. God, a being made of love who can only be approached by hearts that are free, is injected like a serum. We are still at the stage of 'Believe or die'." The Catholic clergy were obviously rankled by such statements and furious that publishers disseminated them.

The first television programs broadcast in 1952 by Radio-Canada, the French section of CBC, also proved to be a watershed in changing public opinion in Quebec. The outside world could now be seen from people's living rooms. Another French-language network, *Télé-Métropole*, began broadcasting in 1961 and provided an outlet for a more popular aspect of Quebec culture. Duplessis had foreseen the role that radio would play when he passed a law in 1945 creating Radio-Québec, now known as Télé-Québec, but no concrete action was taken at that time.

The world of culture and education was seriously shaken up when the Massey Commission report was tabled on June 1, 1951. The Royal Commission on Development in the Arts, Letters and Sciences was chaired by Vincent Massey, Chancellor of the University of Toronto, and by the Dominican father Georges-Henri Lévesque, Dean of the Faculty of Social Sciences at Université Laval in Quebec City. Georges-Henri Lévesque was one of Duplessis's personal foes. The Massey

Commission members made a clear distinction in their report between education and culture. Education was recognized as being the exclusive jurisdiction of the provinces, whereas culture was considered a responsibility to be shared by the different levels of government. They concluded that universities were the main centres of cultural development in Canada. As a result universities could be included in federal policies and be subsidized by the central government. Ottawa welcomed the report and offered to fund the universities. The Union nationale government refused to tolerate this type of federal intervention. Thus began the "subsidy war" that lasted nearly a decade. Search for a satisfactory settlement constantly ran into obstacles. On February 16, 1953 Maurice Duplessis declared: "This year and in the future we will not accept Ottawa subsidizing education, an area that is so important for us. Ottawa's new budget announced new funding to universities. We will not agree with that." An "honourable settlement" was only found in 1960 under the governments of Antonio Barrette and Jean Lesage.

The other Canadian provinces were not necessarily opposed to the federal government becoming involved in certain areas of provincial jurisdiction, but Quebec considered itself to be a distinct society and thus it was not going to put up with federal intervention. Louis Saint-Laurent, who was a Liberal Prime Minister from Quebec, maintained that his home province was no different from the others. "It is said that the Province of Quebec is different from the others," he declared. "I do not share that opinion; I believe that the Province of Quebec can be a province like the others. [...] As long as I remain Prime Minister, the federal government will not recognize that the provinces are more important than the whole country." The year 1954 was another watershed year in the war of words between Quebec and Ottawa as Quebec decided to levy provincial income taxes. Agreement on the percentage of income tax to go to Quebec was only reached two years later in February 1956.

As years went by Quebecers realized not only that the Union nationale government was aging but also that it was up to its ears in patronage and corruption. Government contracts were obtained with the proviso that the party would also get its commission. Known liberals could not dream of getting a job in the civil service where favouritism ruled. During elections votes were bought and absent or deceased people were known to vote by means of "telegraphs." After the 1956 elections that returned the Union nationale to power in Quebec City, two priests, Louis O'Neill and Gérard Dion, published an incriminating letter addressed to their contemporaries. "The wave of stupidity and immorality that Quebec has just witnessed should leave no lucid Catholic indifferent. The religious crisis that we are going through has never been so clearly demonstrated. Never has there been such obvious evidence of the de-Christianization at work among the popular masses." A drop in religious participation had already been observed in Quebec, and this trend began to look like a tidal wave in the 1960s.

Duplessis's government had become a one-man operation. When a scandal broke out in 1958 involving several ministers in his government, he felt that he had been betrayed. A year later, on September 7, 1959, Maurice Duplessis died suddenly while on an official visit to mining operations near Schefferville in the Ungava Peninsula. Many people saw his death as the end of a reign, which Liberals and some contributors to the review *Cité libre* described as the *Grande noirceur* or Great Darkness. Recent studies have begun to cast light on what has been called "darkness." It cannot be denied that Duplessis was an authoritarian leader, who hated trade unions and considered communists and Jehovah's Witnesses to be a threat to French Canadian Catholic society. He also wanted leading members of the clergy to obey him and was known to boast that "bishops ate from his hand." On the positive side, however, he established the basis of an infrastructure that would enable the Liberal government under Jean Lesage to create a more modern education and health care system. Under the Union nationale Quebec built hundreds of schools and dozens of hospitals that proved to be of utmost importance when subsequent reforms were adopted. Duplessis's attitude with respect to business opened the way to a certain kind of economic liberalism and to some prosperity. When he died Quebec's public debt was virtually non-existent.

On September 11, 1959 Paul Sauvé became Quebec's 21st premier. He had a weighty legacy to shoulder, but he showed that he intended to break with his predecessor by using the slogan "Désormais" (from now on). The hope he inspired was short lived as he died suddenly 113 days later. Many people saw his death as a tragedy. His successor was Antonio Barette who left no lasting impression. General elections were called for June 22, 1960, two years after Jean Lesage, a former federal cabinet minister, had become leader of the Quebec Liberal Party. Sensing that times were changing, he made change the leading campaign issue with the slogan "C'est le temps que ça change" (It's time for a change). Lesage managed to recruit several excellent candidates including the journalist and popular television personality René Lévesque and the lawyer Paul Gérin-Lajoie, both of whom became pillars in Lesage's "équipe du tonnerre" or "thunder squad." The Liberal Party program had been drafted mainly by Georges-Émile Lapalme. The program called for creation of a cultural affairs ministry, free education at all levels including university, a royal commission on education, an economic orientation council, a ministry responsible for federal-provincial relations, and much more.

After a bitterly fought campaign, the Liberal Party came out on top. Since Premier Lesage had already been a minister in the federal government, some people were worried that it meant an end to Quebec's autonomy. Barely a month after taking over in Quebec City, however, Lesage participated in a federal-provincial conference and he made his position clear. He demanded full sovereignty in the areas under Quebec's jurisdiction. Relations between Quebec and Ottawa improved nonetheless, and in 1961 Quebec agreed to participate in the federal hospital insurance plan. The Lesage government was determined to assume and assert its role in all areas in its jurisdiction, be it in Quebec or abroad. In this vein it reactivated or inaugurated Quebec Government Offices, or *Délégations générales du Québec*, in New York, and Paris in 1961 and, one year later, in London. This policy of asserting Quebec's jurisdiction at home and abroad became known as the Gérin-Lajoie doctrine, named after Quebec's minister of education.

As the 1950s drew to an end and in the early 1960s, French Canadian nationalism was undergoing a profound transformation with some nationalists openly calling for Quebec independence. Raymond Barbeau founded the *Alliance laurentienne* in 1957. Later he outlined the organization's goals. "The *Alliance laurentienne* is a patriotic movement founded on January 25, 1957 in order to disseminate the idea of Quebec independence and to proclaim the Republic of Laurentie." He saw that the "Laurentien government would be a unitary, democratic, corporative, communitarian republic of Christian inspiration." This new political formation was seen by many to be right wing and reactionary. On the other extreme a group of left-wing indépendantistes rallied around Raoul Roy and the *Revue socialiste.* This group fought for the liberation of French Canadians who they considered to be an "oppressed and colonized people." A much more popular independence movement was founded in September 1960 known as the *Rassemblement pour l'indépendance nationale* or RIN led by André d'Allemagne and Pierre Bourgault. This group saw itself as a movement and not a political party, which it did become a few years later. The RIN was inspired by the freedom movements in former colonies in Africa and Asia. The example of Algeria was particularly important for leaders in the RIN. The RIN's objectives were set forth on June 24, 1961 by its Vice President, Marcel Chaput. "For the recognition of French as the only official and compulsory language in Quebec—for representation by Quebec at the United Nations, the Vatican, and all the major capitals in the world—[...] for complete control of Quebec's economic destiny and its natural resources based on Quebec's superior interests—for the enjoyment of all the rights and all the prerogatives of free nations—for a policy of defence and promotion of French throughout North America and the world. The only solution is INDEPENDENCE."

The *indépendantistes* increasingly used the expression "État du Québec" instead of "Province of Quebec." Jean Drapeau, who had been mayor of Montreal from 1954 to 1957 and who was re-elected in 1960, had already used the expression in March 1959 when he declared: "Finally, to build the State of Quebec, strong, confident, dynamic, and outreaching, that is the great task that we are called upon to accomplish."

Shortly after the Liberal government was formed it became quite obvious that Premier Lesage and his minister René Lévesque did not see eye to eye on the future of Canada. Addressing the issue in June 1962, Jean Lesage declared, "The concerns of Quebecers are not limited to their own province. They also believe that they have a role to play in our country, but they insist on taking the place they rightly deserve and not only what others decide to allot them." A few months earlier, speaking to the rest of Canada, René Lévesque had confessed: "I believe, and I might be wrong, that we do not need you vitally and I believe that this feeling will be growing among French Canadians."

Quebec was obviously undergoing a profound change in the early 1960s. An English-speaking journalist from Toronto coined the expression "Quiet Revolution" to describe the sweeping reforms that were achieved without violent clash. Attendance at church services ebbed markedly. In 1961 priests in the Montreal diocese gained the right to wear "civil" clothing and hundreds of men and women in the religious orders left their communities. Parishes began to lose their status as the heart of social and recreational activities. Professor Gilles Routhier observed that "In 1965 when the Quiet Revolution was slowing down, legislation on parish corporations reflected this change. From that point on, parishes no longer had the right to take charge of social and recreational activities. They would have to focus their work on their basic mission, namely church services and religion. They had to close down their movie theatres, hand over their recreational and community centres, and cede the playgrounds under their responsibility to the different municipalities." In fact, this legal change reflected a drop in the numbers of parish clergy in Quebec.

A few years later thousands of women left the Church in opposition to the constraints imposed in Pope Paul VI's encyclical *Humanae Vitae* issued on July 29, 1968. The main focus of the long-awaited encyclical was birth control. The document essentially condemned practices that had become current in recent years. The text was limpid: "Every matrimonial act must remain open to the transmission of life." Even though some theologians declared that papal infallibility did not apply in this case, the papal letter was broadly denounced and rejected. Newspapers in Quebec such as *Le Devoir* ran many letters from women bitterly opposed to having their rights restricted. Europe and North America were experiencing a sexual revolution under the theme of "peace and love." Jean Hamelin noted that *"Humanae Vitae* prompted another hemorrhage in the ranks of the Catholic Church. Many activists involved in movements defending the family and other social causes simply withdrew."

By 1964 women's legal status had already made strides. Women had attained equal status with their husbands in marriage and had obtained full legal powers, which nonetheless were subject to the provisions of their marriage contract. Under the separation of property as set forth in the Quebec Civil Code, they could sign contracts and, among other things, administer their own property. This marked major progress for women as they were no longer considered to be minors. Four years later civil weddings were recognized and in 1969 the federal government revised the Criminal Code that had prohibited all advertising of contraceptives.

People of a secular leaning organized the *Mouvement laïque de langue française* and demanded non-denominational schools, an issue that was at the heart of the deliberations of the Royal Commission of Inquiry on Education chaired by Alphonse-Marie Parent, Vice Rector of Université Laval in Quebec City. The most important recommendation of the Parent Commission, as it became known, was the creation of a Ministry of Education. In March 1964 this recommendation became a reality with the adoption of Bill 60, but schools remained denominational. In order to streamline the administration of schools, 55 regional Catholic school commissions and nine Protestant commissions were created. These school commissions were responsible for creating large comprehensive high schools. Secondary school attendance almost tripled, jumping from 204,700 pupils in the 1960-61 school year to 591,700 just 10 years later. In 1967 Quebec created a network of general and vocational education colleges better known as CEGEPs for students who had completed secondary school. These colleges provided free education and included both a professional stream and pre-university education. The other main educational reform involved the creation of a network of universities known as the Université du Québec.

René Lévesque, who was minister of natural resources, called for the nationalization of the private electricity companies. Even though Premier Lesage was not enthusiastic about the idea, he agreed to call general elections and made nationalization the main issue of the campaign. The campaign slogan was "*Maîtres chez nous*" or masters in our own house. When the ballots were counted on November 14, 1962, Lesage was thrilled nonetheless and declared: "It is no longer 'now or never,' this evening, it is now that we are *Maîtres chez nous.*" On May 1 the very next year Hydro-Québec officially took over the main electricity generation and distribution utilities in Quebec, as Ontario had done in 1906 when it created Ontario Hydro.

In order to gain control over economic development, the Lesage government also created the *Société générale de financement* that was to "encourage and support the creation and development of industrial and commercial companies in Quebec and encourage the population to take part in the development of these companies by investing a portion of their savings." Two years later the government, inspired by the French model, created the *Caisse de dépôt et placement* that would play an even more central role in the development of Quebec. One of the artisans of the *Caisse* was Jacques

Parizeau, a young economist educated at the London School of Economics who would later be René Lévesque's Finance Minister and then Premier from 1994 to 1996. In announcing the creation of the *Caisse*, Premier Jean Lesage insisted that "the *Caisse* must not be seen just as an investment fund like all the others, but as a tool for growth.... so it must simultaneously generate an acceptable return and make its funds available for the long-term development of Quebec."

This type of assertion prompted many people to ask what the future held for the "belle province," and this questioning would increase as members of the Royal Commission of Inquiry on Bilingualism and Biculturalism, presided by André Laurendeau and Davidson Dunton, crossed the country to discover where Canada was headed. André Laurendeau, who had been Editor-in-chief of *Le Devoir*, observed that "Canada is going through the most critical period in its history since Confederation. We believe there is a crisis. Now is the time to make decisions and changes; the result will be either break-up or a new arrangement of basic conditions for existing." This opinion published in February 1965 reflecting the two options appeared one month after the launch of a book by Daniel Johnson, leader of the Union nationale and Leader of the Opposition in the Quebec Legislative Assembly. Johnson's book bore the evocative and provocative title *Égalité ou indépendance* (Equality or Independence). "The best way to obtain equality for the French Canadian nation in a truly bi-national Canada," he wrote, "is to immediately prepare the conditions of Quebec's independence that will become inevitable if a new constitution is not adopted. [...] As far as I am concerned, I would prefer to achieve equality through negotiations, without necessarily going through the stage of independence, which involves obviously a certain number of risks that are difficult to avoid."

At different periods in the 1960s, small clandestine groups in Quebec inspired by the armed liberation movements in Latin America and Africa and Black liberation movements in the United States began using violent means to achieve their objectives. Successive groups calling themselves members of the *Front de libération du Québec* (FLQ) placed bombs in places that symbolized what they saw as the colonial oppression of Quebec, particularly in 1963, 1965, and 1968. Illegal armed action would reach a climax with two kidnappings in October 1970. Pierre Vallières' book *Nègres blancs d'Amérique* (*White Niggers of America*) published in 1968 became a sort of rallying cry not only for the small number of people who were resorting to violence but also for many who belonged to the post-war generation.

Daniel Johnson won a surprise victory in the 1966 general elections that raised eyebrows in Ottawa because it put the issue of Quebec independence onto the front burner. Johnson felt the need to clarify his position in October 1966. "If Quebec separates from Canada, it will be because we will have been forced to do so. Deep down, no French Canadians want to shut themselves into a ghetto." Former Premier Lesage now Leader of the Opposition seized the occasion to renew publicly his faith in federalism: "If Quebec were to become independent, it would experience the same fate that has struck some countries in Africa that are politically independent but that have no economic independence with the consequence that achieving independence has resulted in a drop in living standards." When some people called him a traitor, he retorted that he "could not accept that people who fought to promote equality within the Confederation could be qualified as traitors."

In the mid-1960s many French Canadians living in Quebec decided that they preferred to be called Québécois. On July 24, 1967 President Charles de Gaulle described them as "*Français*

Canadiens" or Canadian French during his visit to Canada for Expo 67, which coincided with the country's centennial. As he wound up his official visit that took him along the "*chemin du Roy*" or King's way that runs along the north shore of the St. Lawrence between Quebec City and Montreal, the welcome he received was overwhelming. Standing on the balcony of Montreal's City Hall before a large crowd of people waving Quebec's fleur-de-lis flag, de Gaulle made a statement that would resound for years thereafter, and lead to his immediate departure from Canada. "*Vive Montréal! Vive le Québec! Vive le Québec libre!*" (Long live free Quebec). Two months earlier in Paris, on May 17, Charles de Gaulle had already told Premier Johnson: "I am prepared to give you a hand that will help you in the future." Now that hand had been given, but the consequences had not necessarily been foreseen. The Quebec Liberal Party held a special meeting after which its leader Jean Lesage stated that "our party is not a separatist party and [...] it will continue to consolidate the special status that we have begun to build." The issue came to the fore once again in October during the annual convention of the Liberal Party. A month earlier René Lévesque had drafted a working document in which he proposed sovereignty for Quebec along with association with Canada. Another resolution presented by Paul Gérin-Lajoie reasserted the party's position to the effect that the solution would be a new Constitution for Canada. The latter motion was adopted and Lévesque's was rejected. René Lévesque and his supporters immediately bolted from the meeting. One month later the *Mouvement Souveraineté-Association* (MSA) (Sovereignty Association Movement) was founded. The MSA was the forerunner to the Parti Québécois founded a year later.

On the federal scene, Pierre Elliott Trudeau, head of the Liberal Party of Canada, was elected Prime Minister on

June 25, 1968. His outspoken opposition to both French Canadian nationalism and to the idea of Quebec independence foreshadowed the epic battles to come. The following year the Trudeau government adopted legislation making English and French the official languages at all levels of the federal government "where numbers warrant." That same year the Quebec government led by Jean-Jacques Bertrand, who had succeeded to Daniel Johnson after his sudden death in 1968, adopted Bill 63 giving parents free choice as to the language of education for their children. With the massive post-war immigration, the possibility of English becoming the majority language in Montreal was a very serious concern. Bill 63 thus ran counter to the widely supported demand for French to be declared the only official language in Quebec and the language of integration for all newcomers to Quebec.

The Bertrand government's language policy combined with the Liberal Party promise to create 100,000 new jobs explain the Liberal Party victory in the Quebec general elections held on April 29, 1970. In the months leading up to the election massive demonstrations against Bill 63 rocked Quebec. The newly founded Parti Québécois ran candidates for the first time. During the campaign the new party's leader René Lévesque described Canada as a "lunatic asylum in which we are ridiculous, powerless, diminished, and made into whiners for a century, and also we are tragically ridiculed by the old parties that take us for idiots by coining these dam slogans like *Masters in our Own House, Things Have to Change, Quebec First,* and now *Quebec at Work* and *Quebec More than Ever.*" The Parti Québécois managed to garner 23 percent of the popular vote but only seven seats out of the total of 108 elected to the National Assembly.

The word "national" was being widely used to designate Quebec government entities. In addition to the *Assemblée nationale,* there was the *Bibliothèque nationale* and the *Archives nationales* (national library and archives). It would be some time however before Quebec City would be called the Quebec's National Capital. The word "province" disappeared completely from the vocabulary of those who governed Quebec. Only certain "federalists" insisted on using the term province to describe Quebec.

Shortly after taking over government in 1970, Premier Robert Bourassa of the Quebec Liberal Party was faced with one of the most serious crises in the history of modern Quebec. The October crisis as it became known began on October 5, 1970 when members of the *Front de libération du Québec* kidnapped James Richard Cross, trade attaché with the British High Commission in Montreal. The kidnappers issued a press release three days later calling for revolution. "Do your own revolution in your neighbourhoods and on the job." They also demanded the release of FLQ members and sympathizers in prison, whom they described as political prisoners. When the Trudeau government preferred not to negotiate, another FLQ cell replied by kidnapping Quebec's labour minister Pierre Laporte on Saturday, October 10. Trudeau continued to refuse negotiations of any kind. On Thursday, October 15, the federal cabinet decided to proclaim the War Measures Act on the grounds that there was an "apprehended insurrection" and that Mayor Jean Drapeau of Montreal and Quebec Premier Robert Bourassa had requested the intervention of the army.

The army entered Quebec at 4 a.m. on Friday, October 16, 1970. Some 450 people were arrested, most of whom had no links with the kidnappers or with the FLQ. Supporters of Quebec independence were among the first people targeted, including many singers, poets, trade unionists, Parti Québécois organizers, and student leaders. Habeas corpus was suspended, meaning that people were held incommunicado and without charges. Some 4500 homes were searched by the police without warrants.

The idea that there was an "apprehended insurrection" has since been widely contested. Years later, in 2000, Eric Kierans who was a member of the federal Cabinet in October 1970 wrote in his memoirs that he had made "a terrible mistake" when he supported proclamation of the War Measures Act. Kierans felt that if he had resisted "the general hysteria outside," others would also have opposed its use. "Our common sense went out the window, and we gave him [Prime Minister Trudeau] backing for what turned out to be a massive injustice—not merely the military occupation of Canadian cities, but the arrest and detention, without charge of more than 400 Canadian citizens (or to be exact, French Canadian citizens), who were held without bail. They were beyond the reach of habeas corpus, a right wrenched out of King John at Runnymede, in 1215. [...] There was no secret knowledge that explained the imposition of War Measures. [...] It was Tommy Douglas of the NDP who stood in the House, day after day, and hammered the government for suspending civil liberties, and if you ask me today why I wasn't up there beside him I can only say, damned if I know. [Tommy Douglas] showed courage of the highest order."

The day after the army entered Quebec, Pierre Laporte was found dead in the trunk of a car near the Saint-Hubert Airport on Montreal's South Shore. The crisis ended when those responsible for kidnapping Pierre Laporte were arrested on December 28, 1970.

The October crisis in 1970 proved to be a turning point, as bombs and other violent political action were soon abandoned in Quebec. Turmoil continued, however, but mainly on the trade union front. The three major trade unions were the *Confédération des syndicats nationaux* (CSN), the descendant of the Catholic trade union movement, the *Fédération des travailleurs du Québec* (FTQ), affiliated with the Canadian Labour Congress, and the *Centrale de l'enseignement du Québec* (CEQ), the Quebec teachers' union. They were moving clearly to the left under the theme "We must only count on our own means." In spring 1972 during negotiations to renew public sector collective agreements, the three union organizations formed a common front and a general strike broke out throughout Quebec. The Quebec National Assembly passed back-to-work legislation. The three union leaders, under the leadership of Louis Laberge, Marcel Pepin, and Yvon Charbonneau, refused to obey and were arrested and imprisoned for contempt of court. Their appeal was refused and they were held in prison for several weeks.

After holding power for just over three years, Robert Bourassa called general elections on October 29, 1973. His "project of the century," the construction of the James Bay hydroelectric facilities, was under way. The federal government refused to help finance the project. This would be the second election campaign for the Parti Québécois. Bourassa clarified his position on Quebec's future during the campaign. "Separatism must be rejected because it condemns Quebec to be tragically held back in its development and because it will lead Quebecers, and particularly the disadvantaged, to be exposed to severe economic and social suffering. [...] Separatism is unacceptable because of the economic and social consequences for Quebecers, but also separatism with a monetary union is totally useless for Quebec because it would lead Quebec effectively into a fictitious, illusory, and ephemeral sovereignty that Quebecers will have to pay dearly for, and that is absolutely unnecessary." The campaign ended with a massive Liberal victory. Bourassa's Liberals won 102 of the 110 seats and the leader of the Parti Québécois, René Lévesque, was still unable to win a seat in the National Assembly.

Robert Bourassa's second mandate as Premier was dominated by the language issue and negotiations regarding Aboriginal rights and hydroelectric development in northern Quebec.

On July 31, 1974, Bill 22 on "the official language" received sanction. It made French Quebec's official language. Section 10 of Bill 22 stated Quebec's public administration must use the official language to communicate with other governments in Canada and with all corporate entities in Quebec. Everybody had the right to communicate with the public administration in French or in English as they chose. Under Section 13 French and English were the languages of internal communication among municipal and educational entities in which the majority of people being administered are English speaking. Just before Bill 22 was adopted, the Parti Québécois National Assembly member Jacques-Yvan Morin declared: "Due to ambiguity, this law will not settle the language problem in Quebec, but rather increase tensions in Quebec. [...] The bill only confirms the status quo and in an ambiguous manner, just as the current situation does." Indeed, the sections of the legislation on language of education were fuzzy, to say the least, since it established quotas on English-language education for people who spoke neither French nor English.

When Prime Minister Trudeau was asked if his government would step in to declare the law unconstitutional, he replied that Ottawa would not intervene. His main concern at that point was to patriate the Constitution of Canada. Since Confederation had been enacted by the British Parliament in 1867, that Parliament alone had the power to amend Canada's Constitution, the British North America Act, unless that

power were transferred to the government of Canada by virtue of a new law. The rub of course lay with the way in which
the 1867 BNA Act would be amended. Faced with a threat of
unilateral patriation by the Trudeau government, Robert
Bourassa countered by saying: "The Quebec government has
shown its attachment to the value of Canadian federalism
over and over. It does not accept however that a unilateral
patriation of the Constitution by the federal government can
call into question the very principles on which federalism is
founded. [...] In addition, straightforward patriation repre-
sents for all intents and purposes a blunt rejection of the
repeated demands made by all Quebec governments aimed
at obtaining in advance the guarantees needed by Quebec to
ensure the continuation of its cultural identity." This however
would only be a postponement for Trudeau.

While the Bourassa Government was struggling over language, it also had to deal with a major court decision brought
down in November 1973. Following legal action launched by
representatives of the Crees and Inuit of Quebec to obtain
recognition of their rights to land in northern Quebec, Judge
Albert Malouf granted an injunction suspending all work on
major hydroelectric projects in the James Bay area. Although
the decision was overturned a week later, the ancestral rights
of the Crees and the Inuit had been recognized by a lower
court, just as had Quebec's obligation to reach an agreement
with them in order to comply with the conditions under
which Quebec's borders had been extended in 1898 and 1912.
The Bourassa Government immediately initiated negotiations
that led to the comprehensive landmark James Bay and
Northern Quebec Agreement signed in November 1975.

In mid-October 1976 language tensions mounted in schools.
More and more influential English-speaking people refused
to follow the Bourassa government and its language policies.

Adding to the tension, French-speaking pilots demanded the right to use French in the skies. Premier Bourassa decided to call snap elections on November 15. Article 1 of the Parti Québécois program called for Quebec independence after a referendum. This promise of a referendum instead of immediate independence following an election enabled the Parti Québécois to win 41.4 percent of the popular vote and 71 seats in the National Assembly. The Liberals were reduced to 26 seats, with 11 seats going to the fading Union nationale. René Lévesque was ecstatic at the unexpected victory. "I never though that I could be so proud of being a Quebecer," he declared to thousands of supporters packed into the Paul Sauvé Arena in north-east Montreal. "We are going to work with all our might to build a homeland that, like never before, will be home for all Quebecers." Prime Minister Trudeau tried to minimize the victory saying that the "population of Quebec had not voted on the constitutional issue, but rather on administrative and economic issues, which means that Mr. Lévesque and his cabinet have won a mandate to govern Quebec and not to separate Quebec from the rest of Canada." The following day in the House of Commons he drew a line: "We have no intention of negotiating any form of separatism with any province."

For many the time had come to decide.

The Asbestos miners' strike in 1949 marked the post-war period more than any other event and heralded the major changes that Quebec would experience in the 1960s.

On July 24, 1967, the President of France, General Charles de Gaulle, made a statement that has resounded for decades. Standing on the balcony at Montreal's City Hall before a crowd of thousands, Charles de Gaulle declared: "Vive Montréal! Vive le Québec! Vive le Québec libre!" He was forced to leave Canada immediately.

Aerial photo of the Robert-Bourassa hydropower complex at La Grande in the James Bay area in northern Quebec. The James Bay hydroelectric development project was launched in 1971. Following legal action initiated by the Crees and Inuit, the Quebec government reached a comprehensive land claims agreement known as the James Bay and Northern Quebec Agreement.

CHAPTER 11

From One Showdown to Another

The election of the Parti Québécois in 1976 caused frenzy particularly in financial circles but did not lead to any significant flight of capital. The stock market did not crash but several English-speaking companies including Sun Life moved their head offices to Ontario. On November 24, 1976 Prime Minister Trudeau drew the following conclusions about the elections in a speech to the country. "The November 15 Quebec elections have caused anxiety for some and much hope for others. [...] The first observation is that democracy is healthy in Quebec, and that is always good news. [...] The second is that Quebec does not believe in separatism. The Parti Québécois was defeated in 1970 and in 1973 when it was proposing the separation of Quebec. However, it won in 1976 when it proclaimed that the issue was not separatism, but rather good government of the province. Thus, members of the PQ themselves do not believe that Quebecers support separatism and this is more good news in my opinion. The third observation is that Quebecers have chosen a new government and not a new country. Mr. René Lévesque recognizes that he has no mandate for separation." For the Prime Minister of Canada the real and only question raised is "Who can best ensure Quebec's overall development in a spirit of freedom and independence, Canada or Quebec?" The very next day René Lévesque took office and swore "true allegiance to Her Majesty Queen Elizabeth the Second, Queen of Canada, Her Heirs and Successors."

The Parti Québécois leader had never attempted to hide his option and on December 5, 1976 he made his convictions clear once again: "We are going to show the finance ministers from the other provinces and the federal government that we are ready to play the game with them as long as Quebec's needs are met, but all the while we will remind them that the independence of Quebec is our ultimate goal." Tensions immediately escalated between Quebec and Ottawa and were exacerbated when Trudeau declared that if Quebec became independent the territorial integrity of the "new country" would not be guaranteed, thus raising the spectre of partition. "If Canada is divisible," he said, "Quebec is divisible too."

One of the first measures taken by the new government was to defend and promote the French language. Considering that about 50 percent of new immigrants to Quebec spoke neither French nor English, the Quebec minister for cultural development, Dr. Camille Laurin, believed it imperative to adopt legislation making French the only official language in Quebec. The French Language Charter widely known as Bill 101 received sanction on August 26, 1977. It stipulated that French had to be used throughout the government administration, in labour relations, on commercial signs, and by professional corporations. Furthermore, immigrants to Quebec of whatever language were to send their children to French schools except in certain circumstances permitted under the law. The French Language Charter profoundly changed the linguistic face of Quebec. Guy Rocher, a leading Quebec sociologist, wrote: "Under Bill 101, Quebec will never be the same. All those involved, and indeed all Quebecers, were aware of the change. The French Language Charter sent shock waves throughout Quebec society, both when it was adopted and during the years that followed and right into the 21st century. The shock waves were also felt well beyond Quebec's borders."

Over the years the French Language Charter was modified and sometimes amputated of certain provisions following court rulings. In 1978 modifications allowed people to use English in written communication in certain head offices of Canadian or international companies. The following year a Supreme Court decision overruled the section on the language of legislation and justice. With the entrenchment in the Canadian Constitution of the Charter of Rights and Freedoms in 1982, certain parents were allowed to send their children to English schools.

In 1993 under a Liberal government headed by Robert Bourassa, English was allowed on commercial signs as long as French remained predominant. The language question was far from being settled. In 2000 the Quebec government under Lucien Bouchard created an estates general commission on the language situation and the future of French in Quebec. Moreover debate on the status of French has been raised in every session of the Quebec National Assembly since Bill 101 was adopted in 1977. During these epic language battles that have marked Quebec since the 1960s, and particularly following adoption of Bill 101, Quebec has regularly been accused of the worst sins imaginable, including racism, with comparisons being made to some of the most odious political regimes in modern history. Ironically, the effect of Quebec's language legislation and particularly Bill 101 is diametrically opposed to the charges made against it. Thirty years after that law was adopted, people of all origins and all colours living in Montreal and elsewhere in Quebec speak French well, just as immigrants to Toronto or Vancouver will speak English. Bill

101 broke down the linguistic barriers that would have made such integration impossible.

The Parti Québécois government under René Lévesque was active on many fronts. It created a public automobile insurance corporation, cleaned up the financing of political parties, and legislated to protect agricultural lands and to protect consumers. Some complained that the government was becoming too present while others saw it as breathing new life into the Quiet Revolution launched in the 1960s. The population was consulted regarding the movement towards Quebec independence. A white paper on popular consultations was tabled in August 1977, and the following year the federal government adopted framework legislation on the referendum.

The referendum question was made public on December 29, 1979 for a vote to be held on May 20, 1980. The text of the question upset many people. "The Government of Quebec has made public its proposal to negotiate a new agreement with the rest of Canada, based on the equality of nations; this agreement would enable Quebec to acquire the exclusive power to make its laws, levy its taxes and establish relations abroad—in other words, sovereignty—and at the same time to maintain with Canada an economic association including a common currency; any change in political status resulting from these negotiations will only be implemented with popular approval through another referendum; on these terms, do you give the Government of Quebec the mandate to negotiate the proposed agreement between Quebec and Canada? YES.... NO..."

The referendum campaign was very emotional since it often divided families, with some supporting the YES side and others backing the NO campaign. The Quebec Liberal Party and the Federal Liberal Party led the NO campaign. In mid-

April in the House of Commons, Pierre Elliott Trudeau, who was back in power after a short-lived minority Conservative government under Joe Clark, declared that "Canada is a sovereign and independent country and there is no question of negotiating association." On May 20, 1980, 58.2 percent of Quebecers voted NO. René Lévesque was very disappointed when he stated: "the ball is now in the federalist camp. The Quebec people have clearly given that camp another chance. [...] Everybody proclaimed that if the NO were to win, the status quo would be dead and buried and Quebecers would have no regrets." Pierre Elliott Trudeau immediately began to talk of change. "This desire for change must become the basis for renewing the Canadian federation and for giving Quebecers and all citizens of this country once again the desire to call themselves Canadians. I hope that Mr. Lévesque will agree to cooperate in this work to renew the country."

Trudeau's goal was to profoundly revise the Canadian Constitution by bringing it from London to Ottawa. The challenge consisted in obtaining agreement from the provincial premiers on the amendments to be made during or after patriation. Quebec's position could be summed up in three basic points: Quebec's right to self-determination had to be recognized, the new Constitution had to be based on the recognition of Canada's duality and the existence of two nations, and finally Quebec had to maintain the vital powers enabling it to safeguard and promote its cultural identity, specifically in the areas of education and language. Before the provincial premiers had even decided on how to proceed, Trudeau announced that he was ready to patriate the Constitution unilaterally without their support.

The Parti Québécois Government under René Lévesque had failed to win the 1980 referendum but as consolation René Lévesque scored a strong victory—his best yet—in the general elections on April 13, 1981. Although no referendum was planned, those elections gave the Quebec government the "arms to parley" that it had lost in the referendum a year earlier.

Eight provinces including Quebec then formed a common front. However when federal-provincial talks were held in Ottawa, during the night of November 4 to 5, 1981, seven provinces reached a separate agreement with the federal government behind the backs of the Quebec delegation. This event became known as the "night of long knives." Three days later René Lévesque announced that Quebec was pulling out of all federal-provincial meetings except those dealing with economic issues.

The following March the federal Parliament approved the "Canada Bill" and on April 17, 1982, Queen Elizabeth II gave Royal Sanction to the new Constitution that met none of Quebec's demands and provided Quebec with no veto over future amendments. Quebec had been marginalized and found itself forced to live with a Constitution that it had not agreed upon. Moreover, all but nine members of the Quebec National Assembly voted in favour of a motion rejecting the new Constitution of Canada. Since then, no Quebec Government has agreed to join the Constitution that came into force on April 17, 1982 and all Quebec governments have consistently expressed their opposition to it.

Quebec and most Western countries were struck by a serious economic recession in 1982 and 1983. When the federal government cut equalization payments to the provinces, the Quebec government in turn cut back civil service salaries and thereby lost popular support. Tensions were also rising within the Parti Québécois government after the Conservative Party under Brian Mulroney won a massive victory over the Liberals on September 4, 1984. During the election campaign Brian

Mulroney promised to create the conditions that would allow Quebec to sign the new Constitution "with honour and enthusiasm." René Lévesque saw it as an opening and a risk worth taking, or a "beau risque." That however meant putting independence on the back burner. "In the coming election sovereignty does not have to be the issue, neither in entirety nor partially or disguised in any way." Lévesque's new orientation prompted several senior ministers and members of the National Assembly to resign. On June 20, 1985 René Lévesque resigned from politics after being involved for 25 years. With many of its most prestigious members gone, the Parti Québécois lost the next Quebec general election on December 2, 1985. Robert Bourassa became premier of Quebec once again.

At the request of Prime Minister Mulroney, the new Bourassa government set forth Quebec's five conditions for joining the new Canadian Constitution. These were the explicit recognition of Quebec as a distinct society, a guarantee of increased powers with respect to immigration, limitation of the federal government's spending powers, recognition of a veto for Quebec, and input from Quebec in the appointment of judges to the Supreme Court of Canada.

The provincial premiers and the prime minister met at the government's Meech Lake retreat in the Parc de la Gatineau in Quebec and reached an agreement on Quebec's demands on June 3, 1987. The preamble illustrates the nature of their talks: "WHEREAS first ministers, assembled in Ottawa, have arrived at a unanimous accord on constitutional amendments that would bring about the full and active participation of Quebec in Canada's constitutional evolution, would recognize the principle of equality of all provinces, would provide new arrangements to foster greater harmony and cooperation between the Government of Canada and the governments of the provinces." The first ministers undertook to submit the agreement to the House of Commons and their respective legislatures and "to authorize a proclamation to be issued by the Governor General under the Great Seal of Canada to amend the Constitution of Canada."

The Agreement stipulated that "The Constitution of Canada shall be interpreted in a manner consistent with: a) the recognition that the existence of French-speaking Canada, centred in but not limited to Quebec, and English-speaking Canada, concentrated outside Quebec but also present in Quebec, constitutes a fundamental characteristic of Canada, and b) the recognition that Quebec constitutes within Canada a distinct society."

Trudeau had left active politics on June 30, 1984, but he lashed out bitterly at the Meech Lake Agreement particularly in an article in the Montreal French daily *La Presse* and *The Montreal Gazette* in late May 1987: "The real question to be asked is whether we, French Canadians, living in Quebec, need a provincial government with more powers than the other provinces. I believe it is insulting to us to claim that we do. [...] It would be difficult to imagine a more total bungle." Trudeau was convinced that if the Meech Lake constitutional document were to be adopted it would "render the Canadian state totally impotent. That would destine it, given the dynamics of power, to eventually be governed by eunuchs." He completed his attack calling Prime Minister Mulroney a "weakling."

The provincial governments and the federal government had three years to ratify the Meech Lake agreement. When the Manitoba and Newfoundland legislatures failed to ratify the agreement in time, it became null and void. Robert Bourassa felt that these two governments had turned their backs on him and declared in Quebec's National Assembly on June 22, 1990: "Whatever might be said or thought, Quebec is, now and forever, a distinct society, free and capable of ensuring its destiny and its development." Jacques Parizeau, who was then Leader of the Opposition, rose and made the surprise gesture of reaching out to Robert Bourassa and saying "My Prime Minister, I would like to shake your hand." Some people were wondering whether the leader of the Quebec Liberal Party was not quietly becoming a supporter of Quebec independence.

Two months later, on September 5, 1990, the National Assembly was invited to establish a new Parliamentary Commission that was to study the future of Quebec. The preamble to the act creating the commission is similar to the declaration made by Robert Bourassa right after the Meech Lake Agreement was defeated. "Quebecers are free to assume their own destiny, to determine their political status, and to assume their economic, social, and cultural development." The Bélanger-Campeau Commission, named after its two co-presidents Michel Bélanger and Jean Campeau, both business leaders, filed their report on March 28, 1991.

When the Commission was created in September 1990, however, attention was focussed much more on what was happening at Oka and on the Mercier Bridge, which had been blocked since mid-July. The crisis began when the town of Oka announced that it was expanding a golf course on land considered to be sacred by the Mohawks and that was said to include burial grounds. On March 11 that year Mohawk traditionalists had erected barricades on a road leading to a pine grove and the burial grounds. The situation rapidly deteriorated especially when the number of Mohawk protesters increased with the arrival of a group known as the Warriors who were armed and who had been active in the community of Akwesasne that straddled the border between Quebec and

Ontario and between Quebec and New York State. An internal conflict at Akwesasne over gambling had led to the expulsion of the pro-gambling Warriors from that community in
April. Despite court orders, the protest continued. Negotiations
between the Bourassa government and protesters failed and
the army was called in to remove the barricades and replace
Quebec's police force, the *Sûreté du Québec*. The standoff had
escalated on July 11 when the Sûreté du Québec charged the
barricades and a police officer was killed by a "stray bullet."
It ended 78 days later on September 26.

The Bélanger-Campeau Commission ran into some difficulty since its members failed to agree on the orientations to
be made based on their conclusions. Should Quebec be satisfied with the situation that prevailed between the federal
government and the provinces? Should Quebec demand that
the Constitution be totally revisited? Should sovereignty-
association be put in the forefront? Should Quebec favour
total independence? Following consultations the Commission
declared that the status quo was unacceptable. Two options
were possible: the complete revamping of federalism to decen-
tralize Canada, or Quebec sovereignty. In response to a
Commission recommendation to hold a new referendum, the
National Assembly adopted a bill calling for a popular con-
sultation on Quebec's future by October 26, 1992. In the
meantime Brian Mulroney's government attempted to take
the initiative it had lost after the rejection of the Meech Lake
Agreement by holding vast consultations. On the deadline
date of October 16, 1992, two referendums were held, one
exclusively in Quebec and the other in the nine other provinces and territories. For diverging reasons, 57 percent of
Quebec voters and 54 percent of Canadian voters rejected the
agreement that had been reached in the city of Charlottetown,
Prince Edward Island. In six provinces, the majority had

rejected the agreement. Two months later, Jean Allaire, who had been commissioned by the Quebec Liberal Party to produce a report on Quebec's future, and Mario Dumont, the Liberal youth wing leader, left the Liberal Party in opposition to the agreement reached in Charlottetown. They reproached Robert Bourassa for having diluted Quebec's demands during negotiations.

General elections in Quebec on September 12, 1994 brought the Parti Québécois led by Jacques Parizeau back to power. Jacques Parizeau, who had been René Lévesque's finance minister, was determined to make Quebec a sovereign country. Sticking to his campaign promise, he announced that another referendum would be held on October 30, 1995. Lucien Bouchard, who had left the Conservative government just before the defeat of the Meech Lake Agreement, now headed the Bloc Québécois, a political party formed in 1991 to defend the idea of Quebec independence in the House of Commons. On June 12, 1995 an agreement was reached on the referendum between Lucien Bouchard, Premier Jacques Parizeau, and Mario Dumont, who headed a new party known as the *Action démocratique du Québec*. The new referendum question was announced on September 20. "Do you agree that Québec should become sovereign after having made a formal offer to Canada for a new economic and political partnership within the scope of the bill respecting the future of Québec and of the agreement signed on June 12, 1995?" The referendum took place on October 30 and results were extremely close, 50.6 percent had voted NO and 49.4 percent had voted YES. Voter participation was very high, upwards of 94 percent of those registered to vote. Five million eligible voters turned out and only 54,288 votes separated the two options.

On referendum night Premier Parizeau made a statement that he possibly regretted. He said that the YES option was beaten largely by "money and ethnic votes." He resigned within days because he had wanted Quebec to become independent and did not wish to govern Quebec as a mere province. Lucien Bouchard, who had gained tremendous popularity during the referendum campaign, took over as leader of the Parti Québécois and became Premier of Quebec. Prime Minister Jean Chrétien in power since 1993 took a hard line with Quebec and totally rejected the idea of any federal concessions to Quebec. Moreover, the years that followed the referendum have been marked by a continued struggle for the minds and hearts of Quebecers.

The 1995 referendum and its consequences have since been the subject of vast debate both in Quebec and throughout Canada. The history of the referendum and the period that followed it is still being written.

René Lévesque led the Parti Québécois to a surprising electoral win on November 15, 1976 with a promise to hold a referendum on Quebec sovereignty.

On October 30, 1995, Quebecers voted for a second time on the question of Quebec sovereignty. Premier Jacques Parizeau (above) initiated this second attempt to achieve sovereignty. More than 94 percent of eligible voters turned out with 49.4 percent voting YES and 50.6 percent voting NO. Some 54,000 votes separated the two. The history of Quebec's status is still being written.

Timeline

1672-1673	Joliet and Marquette travel to the Mississippi.
1681	Population: 9677.
1682	La Salle travels down the Mississippi to the Gulf of Mexico.
1689	Frontenac begins second mandate as Governor.
1690	Phips takes over Port Royal but fails to take Quebec.
1692	Population: 12,431.
1694-1697	Iberville leads campaigns to Hudson Bay and Newfoundland.
1698	Callière is appointed Governor.
1701	Great Peace of Montreal.
1701	Cadillac founds Fort Pontchartain du Détroit (now Detroit).
1701-1713	Second inter-colonial war.
1702	Iberville founds Louisiana.
1710	England takes Port-Royal.
1713	Treaty of Utrecht (England obtains Newfoundland, Acadia, Hudson Bay).
1718	Construction of the Fort of Louisburg begins and New Orleans is founded.
1726	Population: 29,396.
1731-1743	La Vérendrye, father and sons explore the west to the Rocky Mountains.
1732	Shipbuilding begins in Quebec.
1738	Production of iron at the ironworks *Les Forges du Saint-Maurice*.
1754	Population: 55,000.
1754-1763	Third inter-colonial war also known as the "French and Indian War" in the United States.
1754	Jumonville Affair; the French and Canadians take Fort Necessity in the Ohio Valley.
1755	Deportation of Acadians begins.
1758	Victory by Montcalm at Carillon (Fort Ticonderoga).
1759	Siege of Quebec; destruction of villages along south shore of St. Lawrence; Battle of the Plains of Abraham; Quebec surrenders.
1760	French victory in the Battle of Sainte-Foy; capitulation of Montreal.

1760	Establishment of military regime.
1763	Treaty of Paris; Royal Proclamation; Murray is appointed Governor.
1763-1765	Pontiac uprising.
1765	Population: 69,810.
1773	Boston Tea Party.
1774	Quebec Act.
1775	The Americans invade the Province of Quebec.
1776	Declaration of Independence.
1778	France provides military support to the Thirteen Colonies.
1783	Treaty of Versailles: recognition of the independence of the United States.
1791	Constitutional Act divides Canada into the provinces of Lower and Upper Canada.
1792	First elections are held.
1803	Sale of Louisiana to the United States.
1810	The first bill is proposed to unite Upper and Lower Canada.
1812	War between England and the United States; military attacks on Upper Canada.
1813	Salaberry defeats US troops in Châteauguay.
1815	Louis-Joseph Papineau is Speaker of Legislative Assembly.
1821	Merger of the Northwest Company and the Hudson's Bay Company.
1826	Foundation of Bytown (Ottawa).
1831	Population: Upper Canada, 236,702; Lower Canada, 553,134.
1832	Cholera Epidemic; Jewish Emancipation Act adopted by the Legislative Assembly of Lower Canada.
1834	92 Resolutions.
1836	Foundation of Doric Club.
1837	Russell Resolutions; Patriote rebellion in Lower Canada at Saint-Denis, Saint-Charles, Saint-Eustache; Reformists rebel in Upper Canada; repression in both Upper and Lower Canada.
1838	Declaration of Independence of the Republic of Lower Canada; 12 Patriotes sentenced to hang.
1839	Lord Durham recommends that Upper and Lower Canada be united to enable the United Canada to have an English

majority and to assimilate the French-speaking population of Canada.

1840   Act of Union.

1849   Rebellion Losses Bill; English demonstrators set fire to, and destroy, the Parliament of Canada, in Montreal.

1857   Ottawa becomes the Capital of United Canada.

1864   Conferences in Quebec and Charlottetown.

1866   Fenian raids.

1867   British North America Act adopted by Parliament in London creating the Dominion of Canada; John A. Macdonald is first Prime Minister.

1869   The Métis of Red River create a provisional government; Canada obtains the Northwest Territories held until then by the Hudson's Bay Company.

1870   Act creating the province of Manitoba; Métis rebellion in Manitoba led by Louis Riel.

1871   British Columbia joins the Dominion of Canada; crisis in New Brunswick schools over abolition of Catholic and French language education.

1873   Prince Edward Island joins the Dominion of Canada.

1877   First ice hockey game played in Montreal.

1885   Métis uprising in Northwest Territories; Louis Riel is arrested, tried, and hanged; huge demonstration in Montreal; Honoré Mercier founds the Parti National.

1887   Honoré Mercier is elected Premier of Quebec; Wilfrid Laurier becomes Leader of the Liberal Party of Canada.

1890   Abolition of separate French schools in Manitoba.

1891   John A. Macdonald dies.

1896   Wilfrid Laurier is elected Prime Minister of Canada.

1899-1892 Boer War in South Africa; Canadian troops sent.

1901   Population of Quebec: 1,648,898.

1912   Extension of Quebec's borders to include the entire Ungava Peninsula; Instruction 17 limits access to French education in Ontario.

1917   Military Service Bill receives Royal Sanction; introduction of first motion for Quebec independence in Legislative Assembly.

1918   Violent repression of demonstrators in Quebec City; four demonstrators killed by soldiers.

1919   Wilfrid Laurier dies.

1931   Statute of Westminster is adopted making Canada independent of the United Kingdom; a law in Saskatchewan abolishes French-language education.

1936   Maurice Duplessis is elected Premier of Quebec.

1939   Canada declares war on Germany.

1940   Quebec women win the right to vote.

1942   Plebiscite on conscription: 72% of Quebecers oppose conscription; 80% of Canadians support conscription; foundation of the *Bloc populaire* in Quebec.

1949   Asbestos Strike; the Liberal Louis Saint-Laurent is elected Prime Minister.

1954   Establishment of a Quebec Provincial Income Tax; Jean Drapeau is elected Mayor of Montreal.

1955   Riot at the Montreal Forum following suspension of Maurice Richard.

1957   Creation of the Quebec Federation of Labour; foundation of the *Alliance Laurentienne*.

1960   Jean Lesage is elected Premier of Quebec; beginning of the "Quiet Revolution;" foundation of the *Rassemblement pour l'indépendance nationale*.

1962   Quebec elections on nationalization of private electricity utilities (*Maître chez nous*).

1963   *Front de libération du Québec* appears; creation of the Royal Commission on Bilingualism and Biculturalism (Laurendeau-Dunton Commission).

1966   Daniel Johnson is elected Premier of Quebec on slogan *Égalité ou Indépendance*.

1967   General Charles de Gaulle declares "*Vive le Québec libre!*" from the balcony of the Montreal City Hall; he is forced to leave the country; René Lévesque leaves the Liberal Party of Quebec to found the *Mouvement souveraineté-association*.

1968   Foundation of the Parti Québécois.

1970   Robert Bourassa (Liberal) is elected Premier of Quebec; October crisis: kidnapping of James Cross and Pierre Laporte, Proclamation of War Measures Act, death of Pierre Laporte.

1972   Common front of Quebec's unions and general strike.

1974	"Bill 22" is adopted making French Quebec's Official Language.
1975	James Bay and Northern Quebec Agreement is signed.
1976	Election of Parti Québécois led by René Lévesque who becomes Premier of Quebec.
1977	Charter of the French Language or "Bill 101" is adopted.
1980	Referendum on sovereignty-association: 59.2% vote NO, 40.8% vote YES.
1981	René Lévesque and the Parti Québécois win general elections; Ottawa and nine provinces reach a secret agreement on November 5 on a new Constitution for Canada, isolating René Lévesque and the Quebec delegation.
1982	Official signing of the new Constitution despite opposition of the Quebec National Assembly.
1985	Robert Bourassa and the Liberal Party win general elections.
1987	Meech Lake Agreement; René Lévesque dies.
1988	Jacques Parizeau becomes Leader of the Parti Québécois.
1990	Meech Lake Accord is rejected; Oka crisis; creation of the Bélanger-Campeau Commission on the future of Quebec; creation of the Bloc Québécois.
1992	Referendums on the Charlottetown Accord.
1994	Election of Jacques Parizeau and the Parti Québécois and announcement of a referendum on Quebec sovereignty in the following year.
1995	October 30, referendum on sovereignty with an offer of partnership with Canada: 50.6% vote NO, 49.4% vote YES.

Index

Gouin, Paul, 149
Gravé du Pont, François, 14
Great Lakes, 21, 25, 27, 29, 32, 45, 73
Groulx, Lionel, 81, 144-145, 147-148, 158

Haldimand, Frederick (governor), 77
Hart, Aaron Philip, 98,
Hart, Ezekiel, 85, 98
Hochelaga, 11
Hocquart, Gilles (Intendant), 47
Houde, Camilien, 150
Hudson Bay, 29, 31, 45
Hudson's Bay Company, 26, 128
Hurons, 13, 18, 24, 29
Hydro-Québec, 153, 167

Institut Canadien, 108-109
Instruction 17 (Ontario), 137, 140-141

James Bay, 174, 176, 179
James Bay and Northern Quebec Agreement, 179
Jean Talon (Intendant), 22-24, 46
Jesuits, 16, 39, 108, 131-132, 149
Jewish Emancipation Act, 97
Jews, 14, 98-99
Johnson, Daniel, 168-171
Joliet, Louis, 26
Jumonville, 52

Kalm, Pehr, 25, 46, 48
Kamouraska, 59
Kerouac, Jack, 123
Kierans, Eric, 173
King Charles II, 26
Kirke Brothers, 8, 15
Kondiaronk, 29

La Fayette, Marquis de, 77
La Fontaine, Louis-Hyppolyte, 103-104, 106, 109

La Minerve, 91-93
La Presse, 129, 154, 188
La Salle, René-Robert Cavelier de, 27
La Vérendrye, Gaultier de (family), 45
Laberge, Louis, 174
Lafitau, Joseph-François, 49
Laflèche, Bishop Louis-François, 120
Lahontan, Baron de, 35-36
Lake Champlain, 22, 31, 35, 45-46
Lake Superior, 27, 29, 32, 46
Langevin, Hector, 124
Lapalme, Georges-Émile, 162
Laporte, Pierre, 172-173
Lartigue, Bishop Jean-Jacques, 76, 92, 96
Laurendeau, André, 168
Laurin, Camille, 182
Laurier, Wilfrid, 109, 124, 129, 132-133
Lavallée, Calixa, 127
Lavergne, Armand, 139
Le Canadien, 84-85, 129
Le Devoir, 136-137, 140, 159, 166, 168
Leon XIII, Pope, 130
Lesage, Jean, 160, 162-164, 167-170
Lévesque, Georges-Henri, 159
Lévesque, René, 162, 164-165, 167, 170-171, 175, 177, 181, 184-187, 192
Lévis (city), 50, 59
Lévis, Brigadier François-Gaston de, 55, 62
Lincoln, Abraham, 111
Longueuil, 44
Lorne, Marquis of (governor), 126-127
Louis XIV, 18, 21, 23, 27
Louisburg, 43, 50-51, 56
Louisiana, 26-27
Louix XV, 54, 65

List of Maps, Illustrations and Photos with Sources

208   A PEOPLE'S HISTORY OF QUEBEC